The Most Famous Monuments of Washington D.C.: The History of the Washington Monument, Lincoln Memorial, and Jefferson Memorial

By Charles River Editors

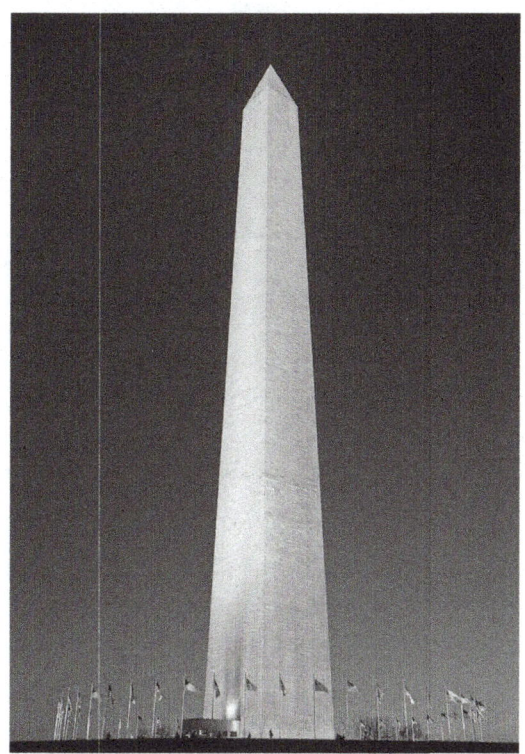

About Charles River Editors

Charles River Editors provides superior editing and original writing services across the digital publishing industry, with the expertise to create digital content for publishers across a vast range of subject matter. In addition to providing original digital content for third party publishers, we also republish civilization's greatest literary works, bringing them to new generations of readers via ebooks.

Sign up here to receive updates about free books as we publish them, and visit Our Kindle Author Page to browse today's free promotions and our most recently published Kindle titles.

Introduction

The Washington Monument

"This structure, dedicated to the first president of the United States, represents the simplicity, honor, and heights for which our national ideals strive."

People have always loved symbols and monuments. Even before there was any sort of written language, there were places and things considered sacred, whether it was the Mesopotamians' ziggurats or the Egyptians' pyramids. Thus, it had long been a practice to make some sort of memorial to those who had died as a way to remember and honor them, and given the importance of George Washington to the young United States of America, it's no surprise that plans to build monuments to him began within months of his death.

There are countless ways that Washington, remembered as "first in war, first in peace, and first in the hearts of his countrymen," has been commemorated across America, but the most famous is the Washington Monument. Congress had actually called for establishing a monument to Washington as far back as 1783, but it would not be until the 1830s that work on the world's tallest obelisk began in earnest. In fact, while the Washington Monument is taken as a given today, and it was designed to be "unparalleled in the world, and commensurate with the gratitude, liberality, and patriotism of the people by whom it is to be erected," there were several issues that nearly prevented it from being a reality, including political arguments, costs, and lack of progress. Though it may be hard to believe, the Washington Monument was not dedicated until the 1880s, nearly half a century after it was first proposed.

By the time it was finished, however, it was clear that the wait was worth it. Soaring nearly 550 feet into the air, the Washington Monument was the tallest structure in the world upon its completion, and it immediately began drawing hundreds of thousands of visitors, who could either climb stairs to the top or ride an elevator. The monument has remained one of the most instantly recognizable structures in the world ever since.

The Lincoln Memorial

A picture of the Lincoln Memorial during President Obama's inauguration in 2009

"IN THIS TEMPLE

AS IN THE HEARTS OF THE PEOPLE

FOR WHOM HE SAVED THE UNION

THE MEMORY OF ABRAHAM LINCOLN

IS ENSHRINED FOREVER" – The epitaph by Royal Cortissoz engraved in the Lincoln Memorial

People have always loved symbols and monuments, and monumental architecture has always been as much symbolic as functional. The pyramids of ancient Egypt were artificial mountains expressing the link of the pharaoh to the gods, and mountains have always been associated with the divine in the human imagination. The Colossus of Rhodes, the Roman Senate House and Temple of Capitoline Jove, the Grand Teocalli and Tzompantli or skull-rack of the Aztec capital Tenochtitlan, the Forbidden City of Peking, the Parisian Arc de Triomphe de l'Etoile and the Brandenburg Gate of Berlin, all provide or provided material focuses for national ideals, beliefs, and culture.

Abraham Lincoln is one of the most famous Americans in history and one of the country's most revered presidents. Schoolchildren can recite the life story of Lincoln, the "Westerner" who educated himself and became a self made man, rising from lawyer to leader of the new Republican Party before becoming the 16th President of the United States. Lincoln successfully navigated the Union through the Civil War but didn't live to witness his crowning achievement, becoming the first president assassinated when he was shot at Ford's Theater by John Wilkes Booth on April 14, 1865.

Given the importance of Abraham Lincoln to the country, it's no surprise that plans to build monuments to him began within months of his death. There are countless ways that the Great Emancipator has been commemorated across America, but the most famous is the Lincoln Memorial, which would not be completed until well over half a century after his death. Lincoln had called upon Americans to bind up their wounds in his Second Inaugural Address, and in many ways the memorial was the result of the country's sectional reconciliation, making it all the more fitting.

In the end, the time it took to complete the memorial was worth the wait, as the finished product included a masterfully sculpted statue of Lincoln sitting in the middle of a giant structure that immediately brings to mind an Ancient Greek or Roman temple. Situated across the National Mall from the Washington Monument, the Lincoln Memorial is perfectly positioned, and thanks to Lincoln's presidency and freeing of the slaves, the memorial has become a poignant symbol for protests, especially at the height of the Civil Rights Movement when Martin Luther King, Jr. gave his "I Have a Dream" speech.

The Jefferson Memorial

The Jefferson statue within the memorial

The story of the United States of America is one of a nation founded upon the loftiest ideals of representative government, attempting to fulfill its goals while encountering competing domestic and global forces. From the beginning, Americans debated how their national government should govern, balancing powers between the federal government and the states, which led to the establishment of the first political parties. At the same time, the nation has struggled to reconcile its guarantee of universal rights and individual liberties with several stark realities, including the presence of millions of slaves at the time of the Declaration of Independence.

Nobody spent more time in the thick of these debates than Thomas Jefferson, one of the most famous and revered Americans. Jefferson was instrumental in all of the aforementioned debates, authoring the Declaration of Independence, laying out the ideological groundwork of the notion of states' rights, leading one of the first political parties, and overseeing the expansion of the United States during his presidency. But for all of his accomplishments, Jefferson's reputation and legacy are still inextricably intertwined with the divisive issues of his own day. As the slaveholder who wrote that all men are created equal, and his relationship with one of his slaves, Sally Hemings, Jefferson's life and career are still sometimes fiercely debated today.

As a result, it's only fitting that the Jefferson Memorial would also be majestic and controversial. A tranquilly elegant neoclassical building fronted by slender pillars and topped by a gently domed roof, the Jefferson Memorial stands among other American monuments near the shores of the Tidal Basin in Washington D.C. Housing a five-ton, nineteen foot tall statue of Thomas Jefferson, the building looks as though it could be as long-established as the White House itself, but it is actually much newer. Facing opposition on several fronts when it was first proposed, including outcries from those who objected to its neoclassical style and others who lamented the clearing of flowering cherry trees necessary to make room for the edifice, the Memorial was finished and dedicated in 1943, at the height of World War II.

Among the countless number of visitors who come to the Jefferson Memorial annually, few know of the checkered and troubled process of its planning and construction. Everything from lofty scholarly debate on the symbolic meaning of its architectural style to protestors preparing to chain themselves to cherry trees to block their felling swirled around the Memorial when it was no more than a set of blueprints and the first stone had yet to be laid. Generations removed from its origins, the Jefferson Memorial is now mostly viewed not only as a fixture of the nation's capital but a fitting tribute to the author of the Declaration of Independence.

The Most Famous Monuments of Washington D.C.: The History of the Washington Monument, Lincoln Memorial, and Jefferson Memorial

About Charles River Editors

Introduction

The Washington Monument

   Chapter 1: A Great National Monument

   Chapter 2: At the Seat of the Federal Government

   Chapter 3: Gratitude and Veneration

   Chapter 4: The Anxiety of the Building Committee

   Chapter 5: A Great Falling Off of Contributions

   Chapter 6: Let This Monument to Washington Rise Higher and Higher

   Chapter 7: Stick to the Original Plan

   Chapter 8: Most Admirable and Illustrious Memorial Structure

   Bibliography

The Lincoln Memorial

   Chapter 1: A Temple of Shining White

   Chapter 2: No Other Site

   Chapter 3: The Actual Building of the Memorial

   Chapter 4: On Reclaimed Ground

   Chapter 5: Two Reflection Pools

   Chapter 6: One of the Most Beautiful in Washington

   Chapter 7: Three Chambers

   Chapter 8: Its Great Beauty

   Chapter 9: The Dedication of the Building

   Bibliography

The Jefferson Memorial

   Chapter 1: Early Washington

   Chapter 2: Planning the Jefferson Memorial

   Chapter 3: Starts and Fits

   Chapter 4: Another Rebellion

   Chapter 5: Construction of the Jefferson Memorial

   Chapter 6: The Statue of Jefferson

   Chapter 7: The Dedication of the Jefferson Memorial

   Bibliography

The Washington Monument

Chapter 1: A Great National Monument

George Washington

Martha Washington

"In the proceedings of the House of Representatives, as reported in the annals of Congress, May 8, 1800, a select committee, of which Mr. Lee was chairman, submitted a series of resolutions directing that the resolution of Congress passed in 1783, respecting the equestrian statue of Washington, be carried into immediate execution; and that a marble monument be erected by the United States, at the capital, in honor of General Washington, to commemorate his services and to express the feeling of the American people for their irreparable loss. ...but for some reason the Senate did not concur. The resolutions of Congress which have been referred to having remained unexecuted, in 1833 some citizens of Washington formed a voluntary association for erecting 'a great national monument to the memory of Washington, at the seat of the Federal Government.'" - Report to accompany H.R. 3021

In 1783, the same year that the Treaty of Paris truly established the United States of America as a new country, there were already plans to erect some sort of monument to George Washington, who had successfully led the Continental Army through most of the war. On August 7 of that year, the newly formed Congress determined "that an equestrian statue of General Washington be erected at the place where the residence of Congress shall be established" and that "the statue should be supported by a marble pedestal on which should be represented four principal events of the war in which he commanded in person." The congressmen even determined what it should say: "The United States, in Congress assembled, ordered this statue to be erected in the year of our Lord, 1783, in honor of George Washington, the illustrious Commander-in-Chief of the Armies of the United States of America during the war which vindicated and secured their liberty, sovereignty, and independence."

Of course, in those heady days, it was easier for the new country's politicians to dream about something like that than to obtain it, and more than a decade passed before anything substantive was done about the monument. Then, on Christmas Eve 1799, the House of Representatives declared "that a marble monument be erected by the United States at the City of Washington, and that the family of General Washington be requested to permit his body to be deposited under it; and that the monument be so designed as to commemorate the great events of his military and political life." At this point, some of those who had previously supported the project sat up and took notice, disturbed at the idea of digging up their recently deceased president and moving his body from his beloved Mount Vernon to a place he had never even visited. However, his widow, the indomitable Martha Washington, acquiesced and replied poignantly, "Taught by the great example which I have so long had before me never to oppose my private wishes to the public will, I need not, I cannot, say what a sacrifice of individual feeling I make to a sense of public duty."

As it turned out, Martha would not have to face this final sacrifice because Congress continued to drag its feet. Also, by 1800, times and fashions in statuary had changed, and the idea of a large statue of Washington mounted on a horse was no longer as appealing. Instead, Congress ordered that a "mausoleum of American granite and marble, in pyramidal form, one hundred feet square at the base and of a proportionate height," be built. Yet again, however, Congress failed to put the money where its mouth was, and by failing to provide funding for the endeavor, it remained unfinished.

After the War of 1812 ended inconclusively, the nation was again bursting with pride, and it began discussing another monument in 1816. This time, a letter was sent to Bushrod Washington, a family member then living at Mount Vernon, asking for permission to disinter Washington's remains and move them to a mausoleum in the Capitol building itself, even though the mausoleum was unfunded and thus hadn't been started on. Needless to say, the Washington descendant was not excited about having the body of his illustrious ancestor moved in such a casual way. He replied in the name of the deceased Washington, "It is his own will, [to remain at Mount Vernon] and that will is to me a law which I dare not disobey." At that point, the House of Representatives decided "that said bill be indefinitely postponed," and the proposed spot where Washington's tomb was to be located inside the Capitol is instead a small vault that holds the Lincoln catafalque, which has been used for the coffin of every president who has lain in state in the Rotunda since Lincoln himself.

Picture of the Lincoln catafalque being stored in the proposed Washington's Tomb

Another bill was brought up briefly in 1819 to build the equestrian statue, but it also failed to gain any momentum. Then, in January 1824, future president James Buchanan introduced the following resolution: "That a committee be appointed whose duty it shall be to inquire in what manner the resolution of Congress, passed on the 24th of December, 1799, relative to the erection of a marble monument in the Capitol, at the City of Washington, to commemorate the great events of the military and political life of General Washington may be best accomplished, and that they have leave to report by bill or otherwise."

Buchanan

Buchanan's proposal ultimately went nowhere, but this time there was momentum behind the idea, and nearly two years later, President John Quincy Adams, one of the few men remaining in the government who had known Washington personally, spoke out: "On the 24th of December, 1799, it was resolved by Congress that a marble monument should be erected by the United States in the Capitol, at the City of Washington; that the family of General Washington should be requested to permit his body to be deposited under it, and that the monument be so designed as to commemorate the great events of his military and political life. In reminding Congress of this resolution, and that the monument contemplated by it remains yet without execution, I shall indulge only the remarks that the works at the Capitol are approaching completion; that the consent of the family, desired by the resolution, was requested and obtained; that a monument has been recently erected in this city over the remains of another distinguished patriot of the Revolution, and that a spot has been reserved within the walls where you are deliberating for the benefit of this and future ages, in which the mortal remains may be deposited of him whose spirit hovers over you and listens with delight to every act of the Representatives of this Nation which can tend to exalt and adorn his and their country."

John Quincy Adams

In spite of this impassioned plea, nothing more was said about the monument for a few more years until a new motivation came along, and fortunately, this motivation carried with it that all important factor needed to get a committee to move: a deadline. In this case, the deadline came in the form of the centennial of Washington's birth. Congress called for the powers that be "to make application to John A. Washington, of Mount Vernon, for the body of George Washington, to be removed and deposited in the Capitol at Washington City, in conformity with the resolutions of Congress of the 24th of December, 1799, and that if they obtain the requisite consent to the removal thereof they be further authorized to cause it to be removed and deposited in the Capitol on the 22d day of February, 1832."

Despite the coming centennial, many people still cringed at the idea of moving Washington's body, and John Washington replied that "it was impossible…[to] consent to the removal unless the remains of one of those dear relations accompanied the body." A Virginian Senator, Littleton Tazewell, concurred, writing, "Are the remains of the husband to be removed from the side of the wife? In their lives they lived happily together, and I never will consent to divide them in death." Conversely, George Washington Parke Custis, the grandson of Martha Washington and who had been raised by the first president, had no problem with the plan and wrote to the Congress on February 14, 1832, "I give my most hearty consent to the removal of the remains after the manner proposed, and congratulate the Government upon the approaching consummation of a great act of national gratitude."

The issued remained controversial until Henry Clay finally suggested that a statue be erected instead. According to Clay, "An image, a testimonial of this great man, the Father of his Country, should exist in every part of the Union as a memorial of his patriotism and of the services rendered his country; but of all places, it was required in this Capitol, the center of the Union, the offspring, the creation, of his mind and of his labors."

It had been over 30 years since Washington's death, and ground had yet to be broken on any monument despite the fact Congress had been discussing one for almost half a century already.

Chapter 2: At the Seat of the Federal Government

"The resolutions and proceedings of Congress which have been referred to having remained unexecuted as late as 1833, certain citizens of the City of Washington, whose names were a passport to public confidence, took steps in that year to form a voluntary association for erecting "a great National Monument to the memory of Washington at the seat of the Federal Government.'" - Frederick Harvey, author of *History of the Washington National Monument and of the Washington National Monument Society*

One of America's strengths is that while the country's citizens believe in representative government, they are also perfectly willing to take matters into their own hands when the situation calls for it. After witnessing lawmakers drag their feet for so long, a group of citizens disgusted with Congress' failure to act on the monument, met to form the Washington National Monument Society in 1833. According to its constitution, "its object shall be the erection of a Great National Monument to the memory of Washington, at the Seat of the Federal Government." The Chief Justice of the Supreme Court, John Marshall, agreed to serve as the organization's first president, and he wrote in his letter of acceptance, "You are right in supposing that the most ardent wish of my heart is to see some lasting testimonial of the grateful affection of his country erected to the memory of her first citizen. I have always wished it, and have always thought that the Metropolis of the Union was the fit place for this National Monument. I cannot, therefore, refuse to take any place which the Society may assign me; and though my advanced age forbids the hope of being useful, I am encouraged by the name of the

First Vice-President to believe that in him ample compensation will be found for any defects in the President."

Upon Marshall's death in 1835, former President and Father of the Constitution James Madison was appointed to succeed him. In accepting the office, Madison wrote, "A monument worthy the name of Washington, reared by the means proposed, will commemorate at the same time a virtue, a patriotism, and a gratitude truly national, with which the friends of liberty everywhere will sympathize and of which our country may always be proud." That September, the Society articulated their hopes for the monument: "It is proposed that the contemplated monument shall be like him in whose honor it is to be constructed, unparalleled in the world, and commensurate with the gratitude, liberality, and patriotism of the people by whom it is to be erected ... [It] should blend stupendousness with elegance, and be of such magnitude and beauty as to be an object of pride to the American people, and of admiration to all who see it. Its material is intended to be wholly American, and to be of marble and granite brought from each state, that each state may participate in the glory of contributing material as well as in funds to its construction."

Marshall

Madison

The first order of business, after extensive organizational proceedings, was to raise money for the project. To this end, in 1835 the Society appointed a number of men to solicit donations for the monument by using the following form: "To all who shall see these presents, Greeting: 'Know ye, That reposing special trust and confidence in the integrity, diligence, and discretion of [the agent], the Board of Managers of the Washington National Monument Society do authorize and empower him to receive from the White Inhabitants of the District for which he has been appointed Collector, embracing…such donations money, not exceeding one dollar each, as they may be disposed to contribute to the erection of a National Monument to the memory of Washington at the seat of the General Government.'"

Two obvious factors stand out about this appointment, with the first being the explicit racism. While it no doubt offends modern sensibilities, it may have even seemed strange to some in that era as well, because there wasn't much sense in limiting potential donors in a fundraiser. Furthermore, limiting the contributions to no more than a dollar each also seems odd for an organization trying to raise a large sum of money. In his history of the Society, Frederick Harvey later claimed that it was done so that "all might have an opportunity to contribute…" It's also important to note that these agents were not volunteers but instead received as payment 10% of everything they collected.

Initially, the project looked like it was doomed to fail as so many before it had. During the first year, the Society was only able to raise $28,000, but this did not stop it from soliciting plans for the monument, which the Society felt should "harmoniously blend durability, simplicity, and grandeur." They found their designer in the prominent architect Robert Mills, and the plan was described in majestic language as the "Description of the Design of the Washington National Monument, to be erected at the seat of the General Government of the United States of America, in honor of 'the Father of his Country,' and the worthy compatriots of the Revolution." While most of Mills' plans, which included "a grand circular colonnaded building, 250 feet in diameter and 100 feet high," were never realized, some of his plans remain familiar to modern Americans, specifically "the lofty obelisk shaft of the monument, 70 feet square at the base, and 500 feet high, diminishing as it rises to its apex, where it is forty feet square; at the foot of this shaft, and on each face, project four massive zocles, 25 feet high, supporting so many colossal symbolic tripods of victory, 20 feet high, surmounted by facial columns with their symbols of authority. These zocle faces are embellished with inscriptions, which are continued around the entire base of the shaft, and occupy the surface of that part of the shaft between the tripods. On each face of the shaft above this is sculptured the four leading events in General Washington's eventful career, in basso relievo, and above this the shaft is perfectly plain to within 50 feet of its summit, where a simple star is placed, emblematic of the glory which the name of Washington has attained."

Mills' design for the Washington Monument

    Of course, it didn't matter how grand the design was because nothing could be built until more money was raised, a process that was slowed by the significant economic downturn the country experienced in 1837. On top of that, the Society faced criticism from those who thought it was not doing enough to procure funds, and these criticisms came to a head in 1838 when the group appealed to Congress for land on the National Mall on which to build their monument. According to Harvey, who published a history of the Society in 1907, "Mr. [John] Roane, replying to an inquiry of Mr. [William] Allen (Ohio), stated that the sum collected by the Society was about $30,000 which was put out at interest. To this Mr. Allen answered that he believed they had collected more than that sum in his own State. Mr. [James] Bayard thought that to erect the Monument on the place proposed would be to destroy the whole plan of the mall, and that as far as the prospect was concerned, nothing could be more unfortunate. ... Mr. [John] Norvell was satisfied that they (the Society) were incapable of meriting the imputation impliedly, he hoped not intentionally, cast upon them by the Senator from Ohio. ... Mr. Morris (Ohio) thought the public ought to be informed why so paltry a sum had been contributed; his own county had contributed over $1,000."

Insulted, the Society sent a scathing letter to the Congress, along with a careful tabulation of all the monies it had collected to date: "The Board of Managers of the Washington National Monument Society, having seen in the public prints a statement that representations have been made in your body derogatory to their character, consider it their duty to lay before you an official account of their receipts and expenditures. They hope that the alleged statement is erroneous in ascribing to honorable members of your body imputations on private character which would not, without proof of their correctness, have been hazarded. The respect we entertain for the Senate restrains the expression of feelings which are not, however, the less indignant for this forbearance. We make this communication in the confidence that it will be the means of correcting any honest misapprehensions that may have existed; that it will be gratifying to a body distinguished for its justice to shield honesty from wanton aspersion within its own walls; that it will afford an opportunity to men of honorable feelings, who may be conscious of having cast unmerited reproach on characters, we flatter ourselves, unsullied, to retract them; that more especially, in case the charges be not retracted, it may be lodged among the public archives as evidence as well of their unfounded nature as of the fidelity with which we have discharged duties of a disinterested and elevated nature; and that, if it be deemed expedient, it be printed by your order by such publicity challenging any detection of the slightest departure from truth. We indeed not only hold ourselves amenable to the public, but are ready at any moment to submit our proceedings to the most rigid examination which either House of Congress may see fit to institute."

Members of Congress continued to rail against the Society and each other for several months, all the while delaying the decision to grant the land. Finally, in hopes of boosting their funds, the Society briefly lifted its $1.00 per person limit on donations and attempted to tie their fundraising efforts to the 1840 census: "The measures incident to the approaching census present an opportunity of overcoming this last difficulty (the former limitation of subscriptions). It will be the duty of the deputies of the marshals to see the head of every family; and as the greater portion of their time will be consumed in traveling from one dwelling to another, it is thought that but little additional time will be occupied in submitting a subscription paper for this object at each dwelling and receiving the sums that may be subscribed, whereby an opportunity will be offered to every individual in the United States to promote it by contributions corresponding to their means. There being no limitation in the amount, every man, woman, and child will be enabled to enroll their names by subscriptions according to their ability. The rich will, it is hoped, be munificent in their donations, while from those in inferior circumstances any sum will be thankfully received. ... The subscription papers may be headed as follows: 'We, the undersigned, for the purpose of contributing to the erection of a great National Monument at the seat of the General Government, do subscribe the sums placed opposite our names respectively.'"

Based on this plan, the census takers would receive 20% of the money they collected and were therefore highly motivated. The scheme would be considered outrageous today, and it was unpopular in its own time and something of a failure.

Chapter 3: Gratitude and Veneration

"The pilgrim to Mount Vernon, the spot consecrated by Washington's hallowed remains, is often shocked when he looks upon the humble sepulcher which contains his dust, and laments that no monument has yet reared its lofty head to mark a Nation's gratitude. It is true that the 'storied urn, the animated bust,' or the splendid mausoleum, cannot call back the departed spirit, or 'soothe the dull, cold ear of death;' but it is equally true that it can and does manifest the gratitude and veneration of the living for those who have passed away forever from the stage of life and left behind them the cherished memory of their virtues. The posthumous honors bestowed by a grateful nation on its distinguished citizens serve the further purpose of stimulating those who survive them to similar acts of greatness and of virtue, while the respect and admiration of the country which confers them upon its children are mere deeply and ardently felt." – Excerpt from an 1846 brochure soliciting funds for the Washington Monument

All was quiet for a few years as the Society continued working to raise money, but in 1844, it received a major boost when Congress finally granted it land for the monument. Congress voted "that the Washington Monument Society, in the City of Washington, be, and they are hereby, authorized to occupy that part of reservation No. 2, bounded by the Canal, B, Seventh and Twelfth streets, south, for the purpose of erecting thereon a monument to Washington, under the direction of the President of the United States, according to the design proposed by the Committee on Public Buildings, and to aid the said Society in completing the same, and for defraying the expense of enclosing the grounds, laying out walks and planting trees, the Committee on Public Buildings is hereby authorized and required to cause to be laid into lots and to sell at auction or otherwise, on condition that three-story brick, granite or marble buildings be erected thereon within five years from the day of sale, the piece of vacant ground bounded by the circular road, New Jersey avenue and B and First streets, north, and the piece of ground bounded by the circular road, Delaware avenue, B and F streets, south; also twenty-seven lots between the circular road and Third street, on Pennsylvania avenue, and twenty-seven lots between the circular road and Third street, on Maryland avenue, northwest, or so much as shall be necessary to complete the same. The same to be designated as 'Monument Square.'"

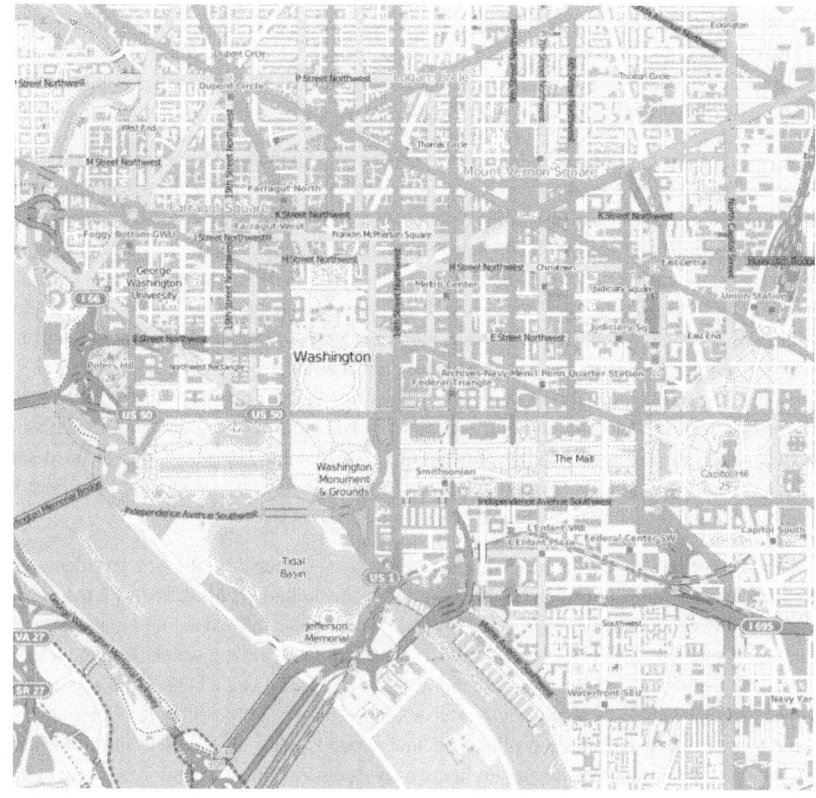

A map of Washington

Thus Congress showed its faith in the work by not only raising money to support it but in creating a neighborhood of attractive homes and offices to surround it "so that preparations may be immediately made [for a] site for a National Monument, which in the course of a few years will become a beautiful resort for the citizens and visitors of the District as well as for strangers from all parts of the world."

The order went on to observe that there would be land for a 52 acre park "to fence in and lay out in drives, walks, and trees, and to erect thereon a National Monument in the center thereof." However, Congress surprisingly underestimated the size of the monument when describing it as "one hundred and fifty feet high," and the legislature also called for the area to be "devoted to the public as a place of resort where busts, statues, and paintings of all the great men connected with the history of our country may be seen." The location was a splendid one, just across the street from the "Patent and Post Office buildings, or center of the city, and but a square or two south of the great thoroughfare of the city, the Pennsylvania avenue, which, in point of magnitude and of easy approach to our citizens, there is no ground in the District, or in any other country, which could vie with it as a public square of beauty and recreation."

The problem was that most of these remarks proved to be nothing more than pretty promises, and while there was now land for the monument, the Society still did not have enough money to complete the project, especially as Mills envisioned it. As a result, the Society decided to remove once and for all the $1.00 limit on donations and make another push to raise the money for the project by using the fact that it now had land to build it on. In 1846, the Society sent out a new appeal "to the American people," informing them "that the delay in commencing the Monument has been occasioned by the want of a proper site, which the Board had hoped would long since have been granted by Congress. The Board designed at as early period to commence the Monument, but as no site could be obtained sufficiently eligible on any other ground than the public mall, near the Potomac, and as that could only be obtained by a grant from Congress, which has not yet been made, that purpose has been unavoidably postponed until the next session of the National Legislature, when it is believed no objection will be made to allow the Board the use of the ground it desires for so laudable and patriotic an object."

The Society then closed its appeal with an eloquent plea on behalf of the first president, who had been dead for almost 50 years: "The character of Washington is identified with the glory and greatness of his country. It belongs to history, into which it has infused a moral grandeur and beauty. It presents a verdant oasis on the dreary waste of the world, on which the mind loves to repose, and the patriot and philosopher delights to dwell. Such a being but seldom appears to illustrate and give splendor to the annals of mankind, and the country which gave him birth should take a pride in bestowing posthumous honors on his name. It is not to transmit the name or fame of the illustrious Washington to future ages that a Monument should be erected to his memory; but to show that the People of this Republic at least are not ungrateful, and that they desire to manifest their love of eminent public and private virtues by some enduring memorial which, like the pyramids of Egypt, shall fatigue time by its duration."

In this push for donations, the Society did two things it had never done before, and both proved critical in its efforts. First, it offered incentives for those donating by promising that the "subscriber of $5.00 was to receive one of the large prints; of $8.00, both the large prints; of $1.00, one of the small prints; and to the subscriber of $1.50, both of the small prints." Also, the Society gave itself a deadline by claiming that the cornerstone would be set "on the 4th of July next, and arrangements will be made to give to the ceremony a national character corresponding with the character and magnitude of the work."

These efforts paid off; by the end of the year, the Society had $87,000, enough to begin work.

Chapter 4: The Anxiety of the Building Committee

"The base or foundation masonry was about 80 feet square at the bottom, laid at a depth of but eight feet below the surface of the ground, and carried up, in steps of about three feet rise, to a height of 25 feet, where it is 58 feet square. The slight depth to which the foundation was carried was due to the anxiety of the building committee to have something to show for the money expended. It was built of rubble masonry of blue gneiss, the blocks large and of somewhat irregular shapes (nearly as they came from the quarry), laid in a mortar of hydraulic cement and stone lime, the joints and crevices filled and grouted. The shaft of the obelisk was built hollow, with walls 15 feet thick at the base; the well, or hollow interior, being 25 feet square for the whole height then built. The exterior face, to an average depth of sixteen or seventeen inches, was of Maryland marble, usually called alum-stone. The remaining thickness of the walls was of blue-stone rubble backing, not the best construction for a building of such enormous weight." – The Science Company, *Science: An Illustrated Journal* (1885)

From the beginning, the Society loved the site it had been given for the monument, and with good reason. As the Society put it in a brochure, "The site selected presents a beautiful view of the Potomac; is so elevated that the Monument will be seen from all parts of the city and the surrounding country, and, being a public reservation, it is safe from any future obstruction of the view. It is so near the river that materials for constructing the Monument can be conveyed to it from the river at but little expense; stone, sand, and lime, all of the best kind, can be brought to it by water from convenient distances; and marble of the most beautiful quality, obtained at a distance of only eleven miles from Baltimore, on the Susquehanna railroad, can be brought either on the railroad or in vessels. In addition to these and kindred reasons, the adoption of the site was further and impressively recommended by the consideration that the Monument to be erected on it would be in full view of Mount Vernon, where rest the ashes of the Chief; and by evidence that Washington himself, whose unerring judgment had selected this city to be the Capital of the Nation, had also selected this particular spot for a Monument to the American Revolution, which in the year 1795 it was proposed should be erected or placed at the 'permanent seat of Government of the United States.' This Monument was to have been executed by Ceracchi, a Roman sculptor, and paid for by contributions of individuals. The same site is marked on Major L'Enfant's map of Washington City for the equestrian statue of General Washington, ordered by Congress in 1783, which map was examined, approved, and transmitted to Congress by him when President of the United States."

With money finally in its coffers, the Society ordered the stone to build the mighty structure, including huge flats of gneiss from the Potomac Valley to cover the shaft and giant blocks of blue stone, each of the latter being no smaller than 16 feet long and 7 feet thick. Meanwhile, Mills himself supervised the work on the foundations, and he told one reporter, "The foundation [is] built with massive stones of the firmest texture, the blue rock of the Potomac Valley, many of the blocks of which weigh from six to eight tons, and which come out of the quarry in square masses, as if cut with the tool, and of varied shapes, so that when laid in the foundation they allow and are made to dovetail into each other, forming thereby a stronger mass of masonry than if the same were squared up as in regular masonry. The mortar used in bedding and binding the stones is composed of hydraulic cement and strong stone lime, with their proper proportion of coarse sharp sand, which will become as hard as the stone it binds in a very few weeks. Every crevice of the stone is filled up with this mortar, and grouted. The square or footing of this foundation for the obelisk is eighty feet each way, and rising by offsets or steps twenty five feet high, the whole built of solid masonry, upon which the obelisk shaft will be placed."

A stickler for safety, Mills insisted that more than a dozen architects inspect the foundation before any construction began above ground, and after they pronounced that "it could not be better," Mills wrote, "Every precaution was taken to test the understrata where the foundations were laid. A well was dug some little distance, which indicated favorably; the strata was found very compact, requiring a pick to break it up, and at the depth of twenty feet a solid bed of gravel was reached, and six feet lower an abundant supply of the finest water was obtained. Though the indication were [sic] satisfactory, the architect of the work directed a shaft to be sunk in the center of the foundation, twenty feet below the bottom of the same, and the same results took place as in the case of the well. This shaft was also walled up, and has served a good purpose in keeping the foundations dry, and will serve a valuable one hereafter in furnishing a full supply of excellent water as the work goes up; as, by means of a force pump, it could be sent up to the top of the monument, thus supplying a refreshing beverage to the workmen, as well as meeting the demands of the work for water."

It finally seemed that things might be going well for the project, and once the foundation had been thoroughly inspected, the 24,500 pound cornerstone was laid on July 4, 1848 amidst much pomp and fanfare. One newspaper reporting on the event wrote that it "surpassed in magnificence and moral grandeur anything of the kind ever witnessed in this metropolis, since the formation of the Republic." Another proclaimed, "The day was fine. The rain had laid the dust and infused a delicious freshness in the air. The procession was extensive and beautiful. It embraced many military companies of our own and our sister cities…the President and Cabinet and various officers of the Executive Departments; many of the Members of Congress; citizens and strangers who had poured into the city. When the lengthened procession had reached the site of the Monument they were joined by a whole cortege of ladies and gentlemen; and we are free to say we never beheld so magnificent a spectacle. From 15,000 to 20,000 persons are estimated to have been present, stretched over a large area of ground from the southern hill, gradually sloping down to the plain below. In a hollow spread with boards and surrounded with seats the crowd gathered. … But its most attractive ornament was a living American eagle, with its dark plumage, piercing eye, and snowy head and tail, who seemed to look with anxious gaze on the unwonted spectacle below. This is the same eagle which in Alexandria surmounted the arch of welcome there erected to Lafayette…. The fireworks exhibited on the same theatre, and prepared by the pyrotechnists of the navy yard, were admirable beyond description. They were witnessed by an immense multitude. The President's reception at night in the East Room was very numerously attended. Thus passed one of the most splendid and agreeable days Washington has ever witnessed."

By September, Mills was able to report that "the foundations are now brought up nearly to the surface of the ground; the second step being nearly completed, which covers up the corner stone," and that "about two thousand perches of stone are laid, and it is expected the foundations will be all ready for the stone work before the winter sets in."

During this time, the Society decided to invite states from around the country to contribute blocks of stone from their own quarries to be included in the project, and this idea quickly expanded to include invitations to other countries around the world to do likewise. As one brochure published nearly a century later observed, "In order to make the erection of the Monument as expressive as possible of the leading position occupied by Washington in the public mind, regardless of class or section, the Society had meanwhile encouraged States, municipalities, and societies to contribute stones for the interior walls. These stones were to be products of the contributing locality, were to be approximately 4 feet long and 2 feet high, and were to bear patriotic inscriptions. Eventually, all the States and more than a score of municipalities contributed memorial blocks. Even Americans living in distant Foo-Chow-Foo, China, in 1857, gave a stone. There are also blocks given by counties of the different States. Foreign countries were likewise invited to send stones indicative of their respect for George Washington and the United States. From Greece, 'the mother of ancient liberty,' came a block of white marble from the ruins of the Parthenon. A stone from Japan, sent in 1853, the year of Matthew G. Perry's famous expedition which opened that country to western influence, was one of the first exports to the United States from the island empire. Stones also came from Turkey, China, and other distant lands."

A picture of a stone from Utah commemorating the Mormon state of Deseret

From there, it was smooth sailing for several years, and throughout the early 1850s, the obelisk grew a little taller each week. By the end of 1852, it was more than 125 feet tall, and in September 1854, the project superintendent was able to inform the Society that "there is now on the ground 835 feet face measurement or about 1500 cubic feet of marble which will make 2 additional courses and leave a balance of 51 feet face measurement which by the 1st of October will be increased to about 150 feet, leaving 240 feet required to make an additional course...It would be very desirable could the marble which is now laying on the ground cut be set in the building as it will be liable to injury should it be suffered to remain on the ground...have spoken to the men and told them the probability of the work being stopped on the 1st of October. They agree should the Board permit them to continue to take any portion of their wages (no matter how small) which it may be convenient to pay them and to wait for the balance until funds were collected, so that by an outlay of say $1000, between the 1st of November and the 1st of December, all the stone now cut could be set in the building, leaving none but the rough marble on the ground which could not be injured..."

As it turned out, it was smart to make plans postponing the completion of the project because the Society had already spent over $230,000 and was nearly out of money.

Chapter 5: A Great Falling Off of Contributions

"The further collection of funds for the Monument was not only curtailed by the destruction of the Pope's stone, but the political and business conditions of the country in 1854 caused a great falling off in contributions. The Monument had now reached a height of 153 feet above the foundation, and the Society had expended on the entire structure $230,000. The funds being now practically exhausted, and all its efforts to obtain further sums proving abortive in this year, 1854, the Society presented a memorial to Congress representing that they were unable to devise any plan likely to succeed in raising the requisite means, and under the circumstances asked that Congress might take such action as it deemed proper." - Frederick Harvey

Another blow to the effort came on March 8, 1854 when the structure itself was vandalized. According to the *Daily National Intelligencer*, "A deed of barbarism was enacted on Monday morning last, between one and two o'clock, by several persons (number not known, but supposed to be from four to ten), which will be considered as belonging rather to some of the centuries considerably in our rear than to the better half of the boasted Nineteenth Century. We refer to the forcible seizure from its place of deposit, in a shed at the Washington Monument, of a block of marble sent hither from Rome, a tribute to the memory of Washington by the Pontiff, and intended to become a part of the edifice now erecting to signalize his name and glory. It originally stood in the Temple of Concord at Rome, was of beautiful texture, and had for its dimensions a length of three feet, height of eighteen inches, and thickness of ten inches."

Still seething, the reporter continued, "The account we hear of the matter is this: That at about the time above mentioned several men suddenly surrounded the watch box of the night watchman, and passed a cord, such as is used for clothes lines, around the box, and piled stones against the door, calling to the man within that if he kept quiet he would not be injured, at the same time they pasted pieces of newspapers on the two or three window openings that commanded the particular shed containing the fated block, so as to prevent the watchman from seeing their operations. They then removed one of the strips in front of the place where the block stood, and passing in and out by the opening carried it off by placing it on a hand cart used about the premises. There is no doubt they took the block to the river side, not less than a quarter of a mile off, and pitched it over the steep bank upon the river beach, where they enjoyed a favorable opportunity of breaking it up undiscovered or boating it off into the river, which they probably did after defacing it."

One of the most disturbing aspects of the account was that it could have been an inside job. Anti-Catholic sentiment ran high in 19th century America, and it's altogether possible that many were offended that an American monument was using a gift obtained from the Pope. In fact, the Society had received many petitions protesting the gift, with one saying, "We, the undersigned, citizens…the State of New Jersey, believing the proffer of a block of marble recently made by the Pope of Rome to this country for the Washington Monument to be totally inconsistent with the known principles of that despotic system of government of which he is the head; that the inscription, 'Rome to America,' engraved upon it, bears a significance beyond its natural meaning; that the construction is an artful stratagem, calculated to divert the attention of the American people for the present from his animosity to republican institutions by an outward profession of regard; that the gift of a despot, if placed within those walls, can never be looked upon by true Americans but with feelings of mortification and disgust; and believing that the original design of the structure was to perpetuate the memory of Washington as the champion of American liberty, its national character should be preserved, do therefore most earnestly protest against the placing of said stone within the Monument, or any other stone from any other than a republican government."

The *Intelligencer* article concluded, "All this went on, it seems, without effective remonstrance from the watchman, although he had with him a double-barrel shot gun loaded with buck shot, and the operations at the shed were within easy shot. As for the pasting on the windows, there was nothing in that, for they slid up and down like the sashes of an omnibus. These proceedings, the watchman says, took place about half-past one; but he gave no notice of it to the family residing at the Monument until four. For these and other similar reasons he has been suspended."

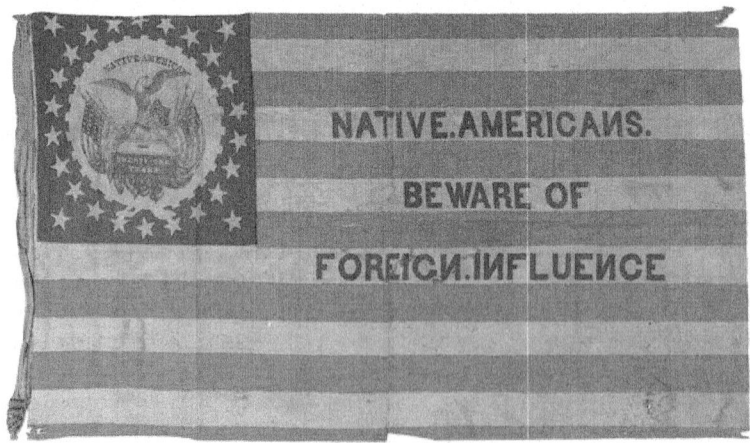

Picture of a "Know-Nothing" flag

The scandal surrounding the vandalism only increased the Society's difficulty raising money. In addition to regional differences between the North and South, strict lines were drawn between those with differing religious beliefs. The Catholics were angry that the stone had been taken, while the Protestants were angry that it was there in the first place. These factors, combined with another economic downturn, led the Society to appeal to Congress for $200,000 to keep the work going. In doing so, it reminded that august body that $200,000 was no more than what Congress had originally pledged to a memorial back in 1801.

At first, it looked that the Society might get its money. One politician praised the efforts thus far: "The Society was organized on an admirable plan, and its officers undertook the duties assigned them by its Constitution, and have, as your committee are well satisfied, faithfully performed them. ... It may well be questioned if any Society executing a plan for collecting money so extensively has met with equal success in justifying the integrity of its agents, and it is pleasing to state that not one cent of the funds received by the Society has at any time been lost by investment or otherwise."

However, the Society that he was talking about was actually on the verge of collapse, as anti-Catholic feelings and political conflicts began to break it in half. On February 22, 1855, a group of members met secretly and voted into office a new board of directors, all of them members of the rising "Know-Nothing Party." They were committed to completing the monument their own way, writing, "It was an American Monument, and its construction and management was said to be mainly in the hands of Catholics and foreigners. Complaints were also made of the administration of the association, and of the expenditures and losses in the collections of funds. For these and divers other causes, the Americans of this District resolved in their respective Councils that this work ought to be typical of their Government, completed by the free act of the People, under the direction and by the hands of the natives. Accordingly, at the election held on the 22d of February last, they nominated and elected a ticket of their own Order, who now have the control of the work. ... Brethren, it is a national work—it is the heaped-up offering of mighty people—it is the work of the age. To it, from every kindred and nation, offerings have been brought—the tribute of far-off lands to that name which stands single, alone, mighty, majestic, in the history of the world, as though it were written in letters of starry light in the high heavens, to be read by all men. These are but the homage paid to virtue end renown, while the heart is cold or hostile."

When the current superintendent refused to recognize their authority, they fired him and replaced him with a man named Samuel Briggs. Meanwhile, the original Society maintained that they were still in charge, leading to a battle for control lasting nearly 3 years, during which almost no work was done on the monument. Finally, in 1859, the Know-Nothing members gave up control of the Society and Congress formally incorporated the remaining organization, preventing similar power plays in the future.

Of course, by this time, it was too late for anything substantive to be done on the monument before the Civil War broke out. For the next 15 years, the half-finished monument would bear silent witness to a country torn asunder and trying to piece itself back together.

Matthew Brady's picture of the Washington Monument circa 1860

Chapter 6: Let This Monument to Washington Rise Higher and Higher

"I hope and trust the work will soon be completed. I hope and trust if there are any States which have not yet contributed and placed their pledges in that Monument of the Union bearing their inscription, it will go on until all the States have done so. I will here remark, it will continue to go on notwithstanding we have disturbed relations of some of the States to the Federal Government; that it will continue to go on until those relations are harmonized and our Union again be complete. Let us restore the Union, and let us proceed with the Monument as its symbol until it shall contain the pledge of all the States of the Union. Let us go on with this great work; let us complete it at the earliest moment practicable; let your Monument rise—if I may speak in the language of that celebrated and distinguished statesman who made the greatest effort of his life in vindication of the Union of these States—'let this Monument to Washington rise higher and higher until it shall meet the sun in his coming, and his last parting ray shall linger and play on its summit.'" - Andrew Johnson, speaking in 1866 at the first post-war meeting of the Society

President Johnson

During the first few years following the end of the Civil War, the Southern states were too poor and bitter to contribute anything toward the completion of the Washington Monument. Likewise, people living in the North, though not as desolate as the former Confederates, were too distracted to pay much attention to a monument few ever hoped to visit. As a result, the Society continued to appeal in vain to both Congress and the general public over the next several years until finally, in 1873, it was able to get Congress to negotiate with them for funds to complete the monument.

Once again, the committee put in place an advantageous deadline, suggesting that the monument should be completed in time for the nation's centennial celebration on July 4, 1876. Although Robert Mills complained that without the colonnade, the monument would merely look like "a stalk of asparagus," the committee also agreed that only the current structure was needed to honor the president: "This rich and massive shaft, though simple and plain, would be a noble monument, worthy of the sublime character which it is designed to testify."

In February of that year, First Lieutenant William Marshall of the Army Corps of Engineers was sent to inspect what had been built up until that time and was pleased to report, "My examination has failed to show any important changes to the condition of the shaft since that time [of the last inspection in 1859, when the Corps of Engineers assigned Lt. Joseph Ives to inspect the foundation]. The masonry of the foundation courses is rubble of blue gneiss. The blocks are generally large and the work, for this class of masonry, good." He didn't observe any evidence of significant changes or settling of the long neglected monument, though admittedly he only spent a very few days on his investigation before he made his report. He reviewed the record of inspection that Joseph Ives had made before the war, and agreed that "all questions as to the stability of the shaft itself have been answered by Lieutenant Ives, in whose conclusions I agree."

Around this time, the committee recommended that Congress appropriate $200,000 toward getting the project up and running again, but the bill had to wait until the next session, in 1874, to be approved. Meanwhile, Marshall was sent back to the monument to make a more thorough survey of its condition, leading John Carroll Brent of Baltimore to complain, "The monument affairs stand as usual, 'masterly inactivity' the order of the day. Nothing can be done or attempted in the way of proposed Congressional Cooperation until Lieutenant Marshall's report be made, and then only if favorable." While Marshall was able to make a positive report on behalf of the structure, he was also concerned about its proposed height and asserted that going above 400 feet would cause "excessive pressure upon a soil not wholly incompressible." After reading his reports, his supervisors were even more concerned and reported, "We could not…with the information before us, recommend that any additional pressure should be thrown on the site of the Washington Monument."

Reeling from disappointment, the Society decided to at least heed the advice of the Commissioner of Public Buildings and Grounds, Edward Clark, who wrote in 1875 that "the present appearance of the Monument and its surrounding are likely to repel visitors; but, if the grounds are cleared of these old and unsightly objects, they will be attracted to the monument and its museum…" As a result, there was a yard sale to clear the area, with an announcement declaring, "On Tuesday, August 24th 1875 at 11 o'clock A. M. at the monument grounds, I will sell a large lot of wrought and cast iron, wood pickets, fence posts, lot of wood, sash, blinds, door frames, slats etc. etc. also one horse. At the same time and place several wooden buildings, large lot of marble and gneiss stone, engine and boiler machinery etc. etc. Terms Cash." The efforts netted $1,500, which went back into the Society's coffers.

Finally, Congress voted in 1876 to approve the funding needed to complete the monument, as long as the Society would surrender all control over the project, and it also appointed a new federal commission to take over the construction. This commission quickly dispatched Second

Lieutenant Dan Kingman to evaluate the condition of the monument. He soon reported:

> "1. That the stratum of sand and clay upon which the monument rests is already loaded to the limit of prudence if not, indeed, to the limit of safety…
>
> 2. That additional weight imposed at the top of the structure would in all probability cause additional and possibly extensive sprawling and splitting in the ashlar facing near the base.
>
> 3. It is evident that the masonry foundation was not given spread enough to carry safely the weight it was designed to place upon it.
>
> 4. There has been actual compression of the soil to the extent of eight to nine inches, the shaft is sensibly out of plumb and the foundation courses show increasing departure from horizontality." (This last observation was based upon an erroneous sighting done from the wrong bench mark; the board later conceded the mistake, but stood firm in their contention that the foundation was inadequate as it currently stood.)"

Kingman

Based on his report, the commission observed, "It is a great, bare obelisk, plain to severity, a conception perhaps most suitable to symbolize the great character it would commemorate…for these very reasons, exacting in all its parts, and particularly in its foundation, all the perfection of elements and details that can be given to its material and workmanship. The stones which compose the foundation should be strong and perfect, truly shaped and accurately placed together. There should be no yielding of the parts, and no disturbance of the levels. Upon such a foundation, a monument could be reared fit to commemorate Washington, and worthy of the nation of whose foundations he was the chief master builder."

Not surprisingly, the Society took issue with what the Congressional Commission said. The Society maintained, "The great scientific attainments of this last examining board will not be questioned and it would be an insult to suggest a doubt as to their fitness to perform the duty assigned to them, and their strict integrity in rendering a report of the result of their examination. But, Men of Science, of practical knowledge, of vast experience in such matters not biased in any way are of the opinion that the Army Examining Board have made a mistake…"

Chapter 7: Stick to the Original Plan

"Three Generals were appointed to examine the strength of the foundation of the monument. Two lieutenants report on the same; one favorably, one adversely. Well do I remember 40 years since, when a boy in Missouri, having contributed one dollar towards the erection of the structure, and have earnestly watched its progress ever since as occasion has called me to this city. Lt Marshall says that one corner is 1 6/10" out of line at the top. Admit it, what difference does it make? It is still far within the center of gravity and is a matter of no moment. The foundation must be of the very best to have sustained the present weight for twenty-five years. It is doubtful if the generals could do as well today. But again you owe it to the original subscribers to stick to the original plan, and as one Lieutenant is as good as another, to have a third part on the commission whose decision shall be final, we do not wish the monument stopped on a tie." - Charles Wiggins

Concern over the foundation's strength continued to swirl, so on June 25, 1876, the committee appointed Lieutenant Colonel Thomas Casey of the U.S. Army Corps of Engineers to complete the Washington Monument one way or another. After months of consideration and calculation, Casey came up with a way to enlarge the monument's foundation so that it could support an obelisk that rose up to 525 feet. His plan called for it to be slowly dug under and poured with layers of cement until it was actually 12 feet deeper into the earth than originally planned. In fact, the foundation would go down until it was near the water table. Casey also drew up plans to widen the foundation and use buttresses to spread out the weight equally so that "the actual load on the foundation, or the bed of the foundation, is not increased" by the additional height. His calculations determined that the pressure on his new and improved foundation, even after the obelisk climbed to over 500 feet in height, would not be more than 55 pounds per square foot, only slightly higher than that the foundation was already bearing. He added, "[considering] that the earth under the foundation will contain some 35 volumes less of clay, in excess of the voids in the sand, than the earth under the present foundation, and that the new bed of the foundation will be 35 feet 8 inches beneath the surface, while the present bed is but 7 feet 8 inches, it seems safe to recommend this foundation for the proposed shaft of 525 feet in height."

Due to bad weather, Casey could not begin work on the foundation until the spring of 1879, but he eventually was able to describe what he did: "As completed, the new foundation covers two and a half times as much area and extends thirteen and a half feet deeper than the old one. Indeed, the bottom of the new work is only two feet above the level of high tides in the Potomac, while the water which permeates the earth of the monument lot, stands six inches above this bottom. The foundation now rests upon a bed of fine sand some two feet in thickness, and this sand stratum rests upon a bed of boulders and gravel. Borings have been made in this gravel deposit for a depth of over 18 feet without passing through it, and so uniform is the character of the material upon which the foundation rests that the settlements of several corners of the shaft have differed from each other by only the smallest subdivision of an inch. The pressures on the earth beneath the foundation are nowhere greater than the experience of years have shown this earth to be able to sustain, while the strength of the masonry in the foundation itself is largely in excess of the strains brought upon it. The stability of this base is assured against all natural causes except earthquakes or the washing out of the sand bed beneath the foundation."

With the foundation now secure, Casey was able to focus his attention on the monument itself and how to proceed from where his predecessors left off to the top. According to an article written in 1884 to commemorate the project's completion, "On the new portion the space inside was enlarged from 25 feet square to 31.5 feet square, to diminish the weight by lessening the thickness of the walls ; and solid granite backing, in two-feet courses to correspond with the outside marble courses, was substituted for the irregular rubble- work. When the wall grew considerably thinner, marble was used throughout. The thickness at 500 feet is 18 inches. The monument rose 26 feet in 1880, 74 feet in 1881, 90 feet in 1882, 70 feet in 1883, and 90 feet, to which was added the apex of 55 feet, in 1884."

One of the changes Casey made in order to strengthen the column at its heights was to use iron load-bearing columns inside the structure and attach the walls to them in order to benefit from the strength of concrete without worrying about its weight. The article noted this, writing, "Eight iron columns rise in the interior…Four of them are far enough from the wall to support the iron platforms and stairways by which the monument may be ascended: the other four act as guides for an elevator. These columns have been connected with the water bearing stratum below the monument, and with the metallic point on the apex."

One of the most surprising things about the monument was that in spite of the danger of working at tremendous heights, there were no significant injuries during its construction. According to an article published shortly after its completion, "The workmen were protected against injury from falling by a strong net suspended around the outside of the shaft; and, since the resumption of construction by the United States, the only accident has been the breaking of the arm of one of the men."

Since the monument was an obelisk and therefore smooth and unadorned, there were a few major concerns about its appearance. The first concerned the need to match the appearance of the stones used on both the top half and the bottom half. Casey was a stickler on this, and he instructed the contractors who bid to provide the stone that the marble "must be white, strong, sound, and free from flint, shakes, powder cracks, or seams, and must in texture and color so conform to the marble now built in the monument as not to present any marked or striking contrast in color, luster, or shade, when set in the wall. The stock must also be free from impurities that would so discolor the stone as to deface the general appearance of the work to a greater extent than that now shown in the portion of the monument erected…Each bid must be accompanied by a slab of the marble, sawed or fine cut perpendicular to the quarry bed…These cubes when subjected to a crushing pressure between steel plates with cushions of wood, must sustain a pressure of at least 8000 lbs. to the square inch. If the bidder has a chemical analysis of his stock he will submit an authenticated copy of the same with his proposal."

As an engineer, Casey was as concerned about the granite blocks used to build the monument as he was the marble stones that would face it, so his instructions to those hoping to provide the granite for the project were just as exacting as the ones for those providing the marble. He insisted "the granite must be strong, sound, and [free] from shakes, powder cracks or seams, but it is not required that it should be free from stains, unless these are due to some foreign impurities that will cause the disintegration of the stone...Each bid must be accompanied by three (3) cubes dressed accurately...These cubes when subjected to a crushing pressure between steel plates with cushions of wood, must sustain a pressure of at least 16,000 lbs. per square inch...Bidders must be able to show to the contracting agent of the United States, that they have quarries and sufficient 'plant' in place, in such working order as to be able to comply with these specifications and to furnish the stock as desired."

The other main aesthetic concern was how to cap the monument. Mills' original plan called for something of a pagoda shape, with the capstone having sides that stuck out past the edge of the obelisk. As time went on, however, Casey became concerned with the practicality of placing such a structure on top of the already heavy obelisk. Thus, he began to campaign for using a simple pyramid design to top off the monument. According to the same article published just after the monument's completion, "Several ways of capping the monument, or of constructing the apex to suit its exposed position, and secure permanence, were discussed. The adopted design was by Bernard R. Green, civil engineer. Three stone corbels, one foot thick at the edge, begin to grow out from each side of the well within the monument, at a point thirty feet below the top of the wall. They increase in width as they ascend, until at the top of the wall the middle one projects six feet, and the side ones four feet and one-half each. From them spring stone arched ribs, which in turn support the roof-covering of stone slabs seven inches thick. The middle ribs rise thirty feet, and intersect on a cross-shaped keystone; the side ribs but against one another, and a square stone frame some seven feet lower down. The apex is terminated by an aluminum point."

Naturally, Casey had plenty of detractors, many of whom wanted to see the more elaborate, Victorian style capstone that Mills had designed for use. However, Casey found support in Robert C. Winthrop, a powerful member of the Society who convinced the other members to support his plan. Winthrop reminded the Society that the monument "was not undertaken to illustrate the fine arts of any period, but to commemorate the foremost man of all the ages...a simple, sublime shaft, on a very spot selected by Washington himself for a monument of the American Revolution, and rising nearer to the skies than any known monument on earth, will be no unworthy memorial, or inappropriate emblem, of his own exalted character and pre-eminent services."

Chapter 8: Most Admirable and Illustrious Memorial Structure

"For some months I made it a study - a hobby. General Casey skillfully prepared a plan to strengthen the foundation. ... Mr. [Edward] Clark, architect of the Capitol, gave constant and indispensable aid to the work. Mr. [William] Corcoran and others earnestly supported the project of going forward, and gradually all opposition was overcome. We decided that the monument should overtop all other structures, and fixed its height, therefore, at 550 feet. On some of the details we consulted our Minister to Italy, Mr. George P. Marsh. Singularly and fortunately he discovered that there was a rule which determined the height of an obelisk by reference to the dimension of its base; and that by the rule our monument should be 550 feet high. ... General Casey is entitled to special and honorable mention. He solved the difficult problem presented by the defective foundation. To him the nation is indebted for the successful completion of its most admirable and illustrious memorial structure." - Rutherford B. Hayes

Although he was a soldier, Casey was also something of a diplomat and only too aware that while they no longer held any official sway over his work, the members of the original Society were powerful and influential people. Therefore, he went out of his way to cater to them, including issuing them a special invitation to visit the monument at critical moments in its development. For instance, in 1883, he wrote:

> "To the Honorable Horatio King, Secretary of the Washington National Monument Society
>
> Dear Sir,
>
> On Friday, the 16th of November, the masonry and interior iron frame of the monument will have reached the height of 400 feet above the level of the floor of the structure. If that day should be a pleasant one, it might be agreeable for the members of the Washington National Monument Society in the city to examine the works; and it gives me pleasure to extend an invitation to visit the Monument at 10 o'clock that morning (or if the day should be stormy, the first pleasant day succeeding) at which hour I shall be on the grounds to welcome the Society.
>
> Very Respectfully,
>
> Your Obedient Servant,
>
> Thomas L. Casey
>
> Engineer in Charge"

At the same time, he was less tactful and careful of the feelings of anyone who he felt was standing between him and the timely completion of his assignment. One of the problems he faced throughout his work on the monument was union unrest, and these problems came to a head in September 1884 when the monument was just months away from its scheduled completion. A group of disgruntled stonecutters went on strike, prompting his assistant, Captain George Davis, to cable him, "Another strike: Man discharged for carelessly spoiling stone; he denies carelessness asserting blind seam. I investigated minutely. Satisfied cutter was at fault and declined to pay him for four days work done. All hands quit until man was aid. I replied that you would decide on returning to city regarding equity of claim of man discharged. They still declined to resume until man was paid. Gen. Newton approves my course but prefers to take no action in your absence. Suggests that I telegraph facts to you. He would close the sheds rather than submit to bull dozing. Value of stone spoiled seventy five dollars…"

In spite of such setbacks, Casey persevered and eventually reached the final, and most challenging portion of the monument: the pinnacle. The article mentioned in the previous chapter observed, "After the main walls had reached their ultimate height, a frame carrying a derrick mast, which reached to a height of 75 feet, was erected on the tops of the iron columns. An opening was left in the lower roof-course at one side; the stone for the roof run out on a small balcony supported by projecting beams, and then raised to place. When all but three roof-courses were set (in all, some 14 feet in height), a platform was built around the top, supported on brackets resting on the slanting sides of the roof, and carried, in turn, on beams projecting through the apertures for observation left in the lower part of the roof, two on each side; and the nine remaining stones were distributed on this platform. The central derrick was then removed, and a small quadruped derrick erected on the platform and over the point of the roof. Thus these stones, including a cap-stone weighing 3,300 pounds, were readily set, and the apex completed Dec. 6, 1884. A small opening near the top, afterwards closed by a stone slab, permitted the retreat of the workmen who removed the scaffolding."

Finally, the day of the dedication arrived, and it was fittingly held on the anniversary of Washington's birthday. Benjamin Perley Poore was one of those attending the event, and he later wrote, "The dedication of the Washington National Monument, on the 22d of February, 1885, was a fit conclusion to President Arthur's official career. This work had been long in progress, as its record, engraved on its aluminum tip, shows. It is as follows: 'Corner-stone laid on bed of foundation, July 4, 1848. First stone at height of 152 feet laid August 7, 1880. Capstone set December 6, 1884.' The laying of the capstone was duly celebrated. The wind, at the top of the monument, was blowing at the rate of sixty miles an hour, and thousands of eye-glasses were pointed toward the little party on the scaffoldings at the summit. All on the upper platform, five hundred and fifty feet above the ground, spread a portion of the cement, and the capstone, weighing three thousand three hundred pounds, was lowered into place. The tip was then fitted and the work was done, which fact was duly announced by flying the flag at the top of the monument, and by the answering boom of cannon from various points below."

A *Harper's Weekly* illustration depicting Master Mechanic P.H. McLaughlin setting the capstone on the Washington Monument.

Those illustrious men chosen to help place the capstone while standing on wooden scaffolding more than 500 feet in the air might well have wished that the Father of His Country had been born during a warmer time of year. According to Poore, "The day of final dedication was clear and cold, the ground around the base of the majestic shaft was covered with encrusted snow, and the keen wind that came sweeping down the Potomac made it rather uncomfortable for those who were assembled there." Nevertheless, Poore noted that the inclement weather did little to deter the crowds: "The regular troops and the citizen soldiery were massed in close columns around the base of the monument, the Freemasons occupied their allotted position, and in the pavilion which had been erected were the invited guests, the executive, legislative, and judicial officers; officers of the army, the navy, the marine corps, and the volunteers; the Diplomatic Corps, eminent divines, jurists, scientists, and journalists, and venerable citizens representing former generations, the Washington National Monument Society, and a few ladies who had braved the Arctic weather. After addresses had been delivered by Senator Sherman, W. W. Corcoran, and Colonel Casey, the chief engineer, President Arthur made a few well-chosen remarks, and concluded by declaring the monument dedicated from that time forth 'to the immortal name and memory of George Washington.'"

Poore concluded his observations with the evening's final festivities, though he failed to mention the fireworks that later lit up the sky around the newly completed monument. "The cost of the structure has been nearly two millions of dollars, about half of which the Government has paid, the remainder having been secured by the Monument Association. After the exercises at the monument, a procession was formed headed by Lieutenant-General Sheridan, which marched along Pennsylvania Avenue to the Capitol. The President's special escort was the Ancient and Honorable Artillery Company of Massachusetts, chartered in 1638, which had come to participate in the exercises of the day. Two addresses were delivered in the House of Representatives at the Capitol—one (which was read by ex-Governor Long) by Hon. Robert C. Winthrop, of Boston, who had delivered the address when the corner-stone was laid in 1848, and the other by Hon. John W. Daniel, of Virginia. In the evening the Ancient and Honorable Artillery attended a special reception at the White House, reciprocatory of courtesies extended by the corps to President Arthur, one of its honorary members."

Naturally, there were some who would never be satisfied with the outcome of the structure, including one particularly unkind individual who wrote of Casey's work to improve the foundation that "it is ... to be regretted that ages are likely to elapse before the monument will fall down." Still mourning the omission of Mill's elaborately designed Victorian style base, he added, "There is some satisfaction in reflecting that the United States now possesses the tallest building in the new world, but this cheap glory will not last long, and when it is gone there will be little else about the monument to be proud of. It is curious to see how completely the original design of the monument has been forgotten. As a part of Mills's novel and thoroughly classical conception, the obelisk, rising from the stupendous colonnade which supported it, was well-proportioned and elegant, but without that support it is an ugly chimney, and nothing more; and the ridiculous attempts which have been made ever since Mills's design was abandoned to argue people into the idea that the monument, as it now stands, is beautiful, or symbolic, or Egyptian, or anything else but a lanky pile of stone, simply illustrate the dullness and hypocrisy which reign supreme among us in regard to artistic matters. If it were not for the enormous cost of carrying out the original plan, with its peristyle of marble columns a hundred feet high, we should be strongly in favor of returning to it."

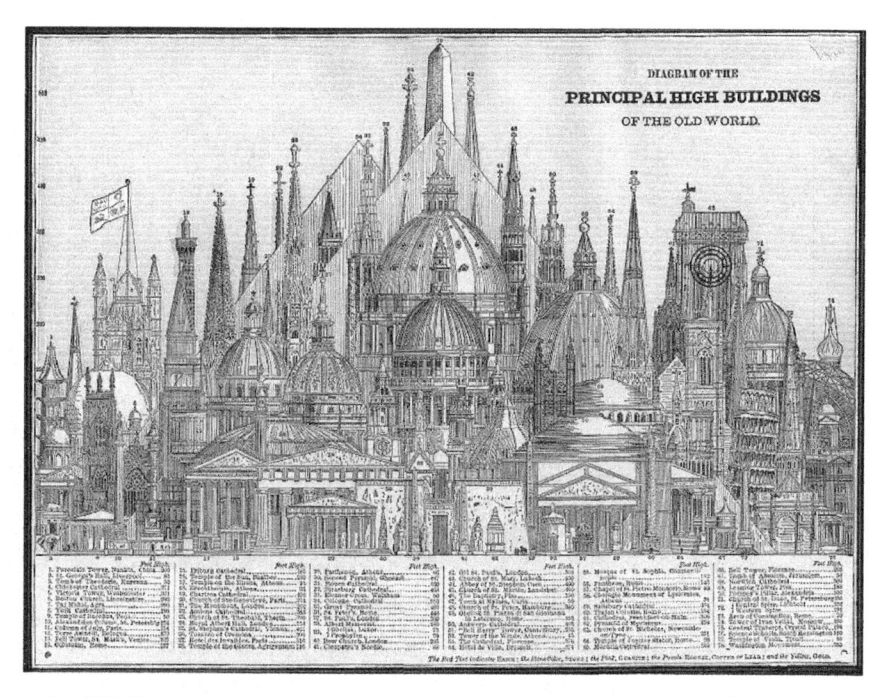

An 1884 diagram comparing the heights of the tallest structures in the world to each other (with the Washington Monument being the tallest)

Fortunately, history has proven that writer mostly wrong. While repairs have been made to the monument intermittently, including most recently after a 2011 earthquake, the Washington Monument remains one of the nation's most popular symbols to this day, "lofty in its grandeur, plain in its simplicity, and white in its purity." Perhaps the most telling appraisal of the structure turned up in a report co-written by Frederick Law Olmsted, Jr. and Charles Moore: "Taken by itself, the Washington Monument stands not only as one of the most stupendous works of man, but also as one of the most beautiful of human creations. Indeed, it is at once so great and so simple that it seems to be almost a work of nature. Dominating the entire District of Columbia, it has taken its place with the Capitol and the White House as one of the three foremost national structures."

Picture of the Lincoln Memorial, Washington Monument, and Capitol

The Washington Monument from the Lincoln Memorial

The Washington Monument from the Jefferson Memorial

A picture of the monument undergoing restoration in 1999

A 2013 picture of the Washington Monument undergoing repairs

Bibliography

Harvey, Frederick Loviad (2011). *History of the Washington National Monument and of the Washington National Monument Society*. Kindle Edition.

Poore, Ben Perley. (1886) *Perley's Reminiscences of Sixty Years In the National Metropolis.* Hubbard Bros. in Philadelphia, Chicago, Kansas City.

Torres, Lewis. (2010) *"To the Immortal Name and Memory of George Washington" The United States Army Corps of Engineers and the Construction of the Washington Monument.* Military Bookshop.

Washington Monument. (1942) National Park Service

The Lincoln Memorial

Chapter 1: A Temple of Shining White

"The last echoes of rolling drums and thundering guns have ceased and civil warfare has become but a page of American history. The broad Potomac River, once the boundary between warring sections, pursues a peaceful course to the waters of the bay. Sectional jealousy and petty differences forgotten, sons of the South now join with sons of the North in rendering patriotic devotion to a government 'of the people, by the people, and for the people.'" - James T. Matthews, author of *The Lincoln Memorial: An Athenian Temple in Memorial of a Great American* (1934)

The site of the memorial before its construction

Given that the Civil War is a distant memory for modern Americans, it can be both surprising and hard to understand that the primary purpose of the Lincoln Memorial was not just to honor the man but to reunite the country. When it was begun in the early 1900s, the wounds of the war, infected by the fallout of Reconstruction and political scandal, had failed to heal properly and remained open sores in both the North and the South. Thus, the steps on which Martin Luther King, Jr. would later stand were first meant to lead to unity, and the vast vista that millions of protesters would eventually parade across was meant to look out on a nation finally at peace. This sentiment was aptly underscored by author James T. Matthews: "On the southern shore of the river, high above the surrounding country, stands Arlington, the home of the gallant warrior-gentleman, Robert E. Lee. To the north is a temple of shining white erected to the memory of the kindly statesman and emancipator, Abraham Lincoln. Bridging the waters between is a great memorial bridge, uniting and commemorating. Time has removed all barriers, and greatness, regardless of section, receives its due of praise and homage. Lee does not belong to the South nor Lincoln to the North; both belong to America and it is fitting that thousands of Americans from all sections should visit these shrines to honor two great Americans."

Ironically, the first discussion about the memorial took place before any sort of real peace had been reached. Matthews noted in his book, "About a year after the death of Lincoln a few scattered admirers sought the erection of a memorial in his honor, but political strife and lack of unity made it impossible to accomplish their purpose. However, the idea was firmly entrenched in the minds of a few contemporaries and they only awaited a propitious time to bring their plans before the public. In eighteen sixty-seven it seemed that this time had come. On March the twenty-ninth an act of Congress was passed incorporating the Lincoln Monument Association. Electing James Harlan as president and Francis Spinner, the United States Treasurer, as treasurer, the Association enthusiastically began plans for a monument to Mr. Lincoln."

The Act itself was pretty straightforward, reading in part, "Be it enacted by the Senate and the House of Representatives of the United States of America in Congress Assembled, That [a number of men] and their successors, are constituted a body corporate in the District of Columbia, by the name of the Lincoln Monument Association, for the purpose of erecting a monument in the city of Washington, commemorative of the great charter of emancipation and universal liberty in America. ... And be it further enacted, that said corporation shall have power to own and control such property as may be necessary for the carrying out of the objects of the association. ... And be it further enacted, that said corporation shall have power to collect money and to make such rules and regulations as they may deem necessary and expedient."

Unfortunately, there were a number of problems with the act, beginning with the Congress who passed it. Following the Civil War, many state and congressional representatives were not duly elected but instead chosen through back-alley deals and rigged elections. Therefore, Congress had little clout with the public, and what little clout it did possess was not readily available to be passed on to entities it created. Furthermore, while the Civil War had been won by the North on the battlefield, it was still being fought over in words by political groups and authors across the country. Lastly, it must be remembered that the Civil War had been outrageously expensive to fight, both in terms of money and manpower, leaving the country too poor to truly build a monument to the man who had led it through the conflict. As Edward F. Concklin, then the Director of Public Buildings and Public Parks of the National Capital, observed in 1927, "An appeal for subscriptions was sent out by the Postmaster General to postmasters, who acted as agents for receiving subscriptions. The money received from postmasters was turned over to the treasurer. Plans and designs were submitted from Clark Mills and probably paid for, but no practical results appear to have been accomplished from this legislation." The choice of Mills at that time might have been seen as a reconciliatory move, as he was most famous for the work he had done in the Southern states before the war. However, since the public was not behind the project, the Association died out with its first members.

As fate would have it, little else was said about the Memorial until the dawn of the next century. By 1900, the Spanish-American War had reunited the country in a way that no sort of legislation could, as soldiers from all parts of the nation fought together in what Teddy Roosevelt termed "a splendid little war." In fact, Roosevelt, a huge fan of history and all things majestic, was president in December 1901 when Senator Shelby Cullom from Illinois felt the time was right to introduce a bill into Congress "to provide a commission to secure plans and designs for a monument or memorial to the memory of Abraham Lincoln, late President of the United States." According to Matthews, "Mr. Cullom was the son of a pioneer who went into Illinois and became a close friend of the Lincoln family. The son inherited the friendship of his father for Abraham Lincoln and was an ardent supporter of the first movement for a monument to the memory of the martyred president."

Cullom

President Roosevelt in 1904

Mills

Unfortunately, the Committee on the Library, to whom the bill was referred, was not so enthusiastic and recommended that it be postponed indefinitely. Nevertheless, Cullom refused to give up, and eventually, the bill was passed and signed in June 1902. According to Concklin, "The act provided that the Commission should consist of the Chairman of the Senate Committee on the Library, the Chairman of the House Committee on the Library, the Secretary of State, the Secretary of War, Senator George G. Vest, and Representative James D. Richardson; and appropriated the sum of $25,000 to enable the Commission to carry out the provisions of the act, the Commission to report to Congress the result of their action as soon as possible after a decision had been reached."

At the Commission's first meeting, held on April 24, 1904, Senator George Wetmore was elected as its chairman. Conklin explained that Wetmore "had previously been in communication with a prominent architect and firm of builders and had secured a detailed estimate of the cost of a memorial, also a statement as to what the proposed sculpture was to consist of." The committee also agreed to send Representative James McCleary to Europe to "gather information concerning important monuments and memorials there, and that he should submit his complete report to the Commission not later than December 1, 1905."

Wetmore

While McCleary likely enjoyed his trip and indeed made a report upon his return, nothing was done with it. Thus, the project languished again until February 1911, when Congress passed "An Act to Provide a Commission to Secure Plans and Designs for a Monument or Memorial to the Memory of Abraham Lincoln." This act stated:

> "Be it enacted by the Senate and the House of Representatives of the United States of America in Congress assembled,
>
> Sec. 1 — That William H. Taft, Shelby M. Cullom, Joseph G. Cannon, George Peabody Wetmore, Samuel Walker McCall, Hernando D. Money, and Champ Clark are hereby created a Commission, to be known as the Lincoln Memorial Commission, to procure and determine upon a location, plan and design for a monument or memorial in the city of Washington, District of Columbia, to the memory of Abraham Lincoln, subject to the approval of Congress.

Sec. 2 — That in the discharge of its duties hereunder said commission is authorized to employ the services of such artists, sculptors, architects, and others as it shall determine to be necessary, and to avail itself of the services or advice of the Commission of Fine Arts, created by the Act approved May seventeenth, nineteen hundred and ten.

Sec. 3 — That the construction of the monument or memorial, herein and hereby authorized, shall be upon such site as determined by the commission herein created, and approved by Congress, and said construction shall be entered upon as speedily as practicable after the plan and design therefor is determined upon and approved by Congress, and shall be prosecuted to completion, under the direction of the said commission and the supervision of the Secretary of War, under a contract or contracts hereby authorized to be entered into by said Secretary in a total sum not exceeding two million dollars. ...

Sec. 5 — That to defray the necessary expenses of the commission herein created and the cost of procuring plans or designs for a memorial or monument, as herein provided, there is hereby appropriated the sum of fifty thousand dollars, to be immediately available,

Sec. 6 — That said commission shall annually submit to Congress an estimate of the amount of money necessary to be expended each year to carry on the work herein authorized..."

This bill was significant for several reasons. For one thing, it made William Howard Taft, the newly elected President of the United States, a member of the committee. Obviously, having the president on board was immensely helpful. Furthermore, the bill didn't just authorize construction of the Memorial but also funded it to the tune of $50,000 and promised up to $2 million for its completion. This was important in light of the struggle that had slowed the construction of the Washington Monument decades earlier. Matthews explained that "the Act named as members of the commission the men who in the past had been the most untiring in their efforts to obtain a memorial. By placing such men as Cullom, Cannon, Wetmore, and Taft upon the commission the Act guarded itself against failure, for these men were capable of trust in carrying out any enterprise and had proven their interest in the task assigned to them."

Taft

Chapter 2: No Other Site

"This site is on the axis of the Capitol and the Washington Monument and is in view of Arlington, the home of Robert E. Lee, across the Potomac River. Thus the Memorial looks toward the home of the outstanding southern leader in the war waged during the presidency of Mr. Lincoln and recalls the services rendered by the former President at that time; it faces the monument to the man who was the father of the country which Mr. Lincoln served, and it is in direct line with the Capitol of the Union which Mr. Lincoln successfully preserved. No other site could have approached this one for appropriateness nor could another have equaled it for beauty, since it is in the section of the city which contains the most beautiful of the city's parks and the finest of the public buildings." - James T. Matthews, author of *The Lincoln Memorial: An Athenian Temple in Memorial of a Great American* (1934)

The first order of business for the new committee was to choose a suitable location for the memorial, and in so doing, the committee wisely sought the aid of the Commission of Fine Arts. Taft, as chair of the committee, asked the commissioners to recommend a suitable site for the Memorial. Their July 1911 report to the Committee suggested the need for a vast amount of land: "This sum [given by Congress] suggests that the memorial is intended to be a structure of large size. The popular idea of a memorial to Lincoln will be satisfied only with a design which combines grandeur with beauty. Assuming that this memorial must be a large one, there are few sites on which it can be placed successfully; for it is important that a large monument shall stand where its environment can be specially designed to harmonize with it, and where the design need not be controlled or even influenced by existing surroundings."

Although the report winnowed down the possibilities, the exact location became something of a controversial topic, as indicated by a 1911 article from the popular magazine *Art and Progress*: "The location and character of a memorial [to] be erected to Lincoln at the National Capital is a matter of national concern. The report rendered by the Commission of Fine Arts to the Lincoln Memorial Commission, which was lately made public, is therefore of extraordinary interest. ... Several sites were considered, but two were exhaustively studied — one near the Capitol, the other in Potomac Park, and of these the latter was unanimously approved and recommended."

Fortunately, the commission was able to give good reasons for rejecting the first site in its report: "The principal reason advanced for placing the Lincoln Memorial near the Union Station, or on Capitol Hill, is that more people would see it there than elsewhere. It is true that more transient visitors would pass it; but it is also true that an object which we must make some effort to see impresses itself on us with much more force than does one which is seen casually or incidentally. Not how many people see a monument, but how great is the impression made by it, is the real test. The locations considered in the vicinity of the Capitol and Union Station are in the vortex of busy life, and whatever grandeur and impressive simplicity and beauty the memorial might possess would be lessened by close competition with the massive structures of the Station and the immense pile of the Capitol. An axiom of Exposition practice, which applies with equal force here, is that the least desirable place for an exhibit is near a busy entrance. Crowds hurry past to see what is beyond. Placed near the Station the Lincoln Memorial would teach but a feeble lesson; and the sentiments it would stimulate would find no adequate response on the part of the beholders."

The report went on to detail just what efforts the men had gone to in order to make sure they got it right: "The Commission have reached this conclusion after having opportunity to consider a set of more than one hundred architectural studies representing work carried over a series of years with the purpose of discovering, if possible, some location and some form of structure which might be introduced into the Capitol area without producing a sense of inadequacy and incongruity. These studies cover the field of possibilities, and prove conclusively that any location near the Capitol presents obstacles that are insurmountable, if the manifest desire of

Congress for a great memorial is to be carried out."

When the Committee chose to put the Lincoln Memorial in Potomac Park, they chose to place it in one of the great and long-developed beauty spots of the city. As Conklin later noted, "The westernmost end of the Mall, as shown on the plan of the city of Washington made by Pierre Charles L'Enfant in 1791, terminated at about Seventeenth Street where it met the waters of the Potomac River at the mouth of Tiber Creek. The reclamation and filling in of the Potomac Flats moved the shore line out to a point beyond Twenty-fifth Street, and the Park Commission of 1901, in its report on the improvement of the park system of the District of Columbia, extended the Mall out to that point and located a site for the Lincoln Memorial at the intersection of the main axis of the Capitol and the Washington Monument with the main axis of Twenty-third Street west."

The area chosen had also recently been drained, which persuaded those in charge that they could avoid some of the problems their predecessors had experienced when building the Washington Monument decades earlier. Concklin explained, "By the act of Congress approved March 3, 1897, the entire area known as the Potomac Flats, together with the tidal reservoir, was made and declared a public park under the name of the Potomac Park, to be forever held and used as a park for the recreation and pleasure of the people. By act approved August 1, 1914, Potomac Park was made a part of the park system of the District of Columbia under the Officer in Charge of Public Buildings and Grounds, who, for convenience of reference, has divided the park into two sections — East Potomac Park, comprising the peninsula east of the steam railroad embankment, and West Potomac Park, the section west of the embankment and extending to B Street north with Seventeenth Street on the one side and the Potomac River on the other."

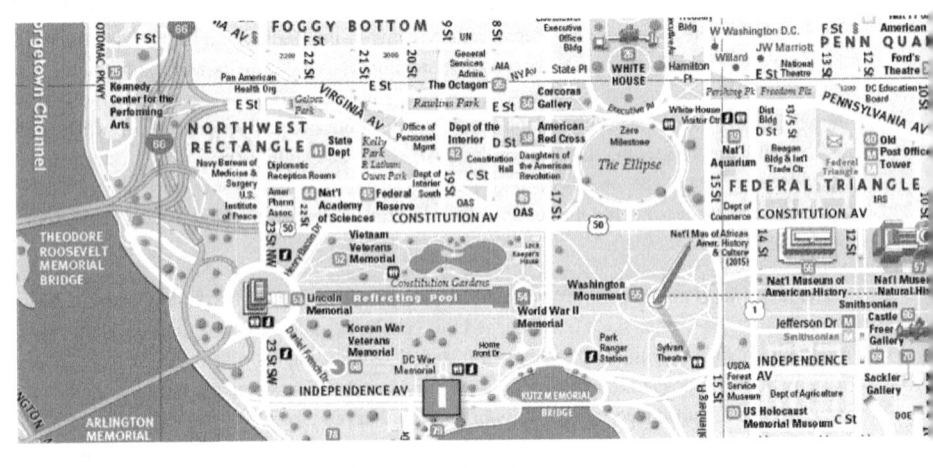

A layout of the city

Chapter 3: The Actual Building of the Memorial

"The site having been selected, Mr. Harry Bacon of New York was selected as the architect for the Memorial building. Mr. Bacon had already created many beautiful structures in New York City and was looked upon as one of the foremost American architects. His selection has been proven a happy one by the masterpiece which he conceived and helped to develop. The...architect having been selected, the Commission and the Secretary of War then turned their attention to the awarding of contracts for the actual building of the Memorial." - James T. Matthews, author of *The Lincoln Memorial: An Athenian Temple in Memorial of a Great American* (1934)

Another virtue of the site was that it had recently undergone further renovation, making it a prime piece of real estate for such an important project. Concklin described it as such: "The first appropriation for the improvement of West Potomac Park was made in 1902. This was devoted almost entirely to improving the area between the Tidal Basin and the Monument Grounds, including the construction of the driveway extending from Seventeenth and B Streets down to Fourteenth and Water Streets, grading the ground along its borders and increasing the height of the sea wall on the north and east sides of the Tidal Basin. Subsequent appropriations up to 1907 were used in grading and improving that portion of the ground lying between the steam railroad embankment, the Tidal Basin, and the Virginia Channel. In 1907 an appropriation was granted by Congress for constructing a macadam driveway on the Virginia Channel side of the park to extend from the inlet bridge south of the Tidal Basin to the foot of Twenty-sixth Street NW., and for improving the grounds on either side thereof. This was completed by June, 1908, and in 1909 north B Street was carried through as a park roadway to meet this riverside driveway. The filling in of the large area south of north B Street and extending from Seventeenth Street west to the new riverside drive was practically completed in 1908, after which grading was carried on with materials hauled in without expense to the Government so that by 1912, when the site for the Lincoln Memorial had been definitely selected, the ground had been brought to the established park grade."

Concklin also pointed out that there was plenty of additional work to be done to get the site ready for the actual Memorial. "In erecting the Memorial an earth mound about 1,200 feet in diameter with an elevation of 25 feet at its highest point was raised around the upper foundation up to the base of the terrace wall. On this mound the Memorial stands encircled by a wide roadway from which there radiate roads and walks out into the surrounding grounds."

While it might be difficult for the city's visitors to believe today, the main concern about the site was that it might be too isolated, something the committee acknowledged when it defended its choice: "The comparative isolation of the Potomac Park site in the midst of a large area of undeveloped vacant land constitutes a peculiar advantage. For a long distance in every direction the surroundings are absolutely free for such treatment as would best enhance the effect of the

Memorial. The fact that there are now no features of interest or importance, that everything is yet to be done, means that no embarrassing obstacles would interfere with the development of a setting adequate in extent and perfect in design, without compromise and without discord. Congress has here created a great park area, raised well above the highest river floods, and this area now awaits development. By the ordinary operations of park improvement it is a simple matter to raise in this area an eminence suited to the site of a great memorial, and to adorn and surround it by such landscape features as shall give it effective and beautiful support. In judging the site of a memorial to endure throughout the ages we must regard not what the location was, not what it is today, but what it can be made for all time to come. The short period required for grading and the growth of trees would be as nothing compared with the possibility which this site presents of treating freely every element of the surroundings in the best manner that the skill of man can devise."

In evaluating the committee's decision, it is important to keep in mind that the Washington Monument had only itself been completed a few decades earlier and had nearly proven to be a disaster due to the low nature of the land on which it was built. Therefore, the more practical minded among the commission knew that Lincoln Memorial needed to be on higher ground. At the same time, it was important that it not be so high that it would symbolically suggest the 16th president was looking down on the 1st. The commission addressed this concern as well, writing, "A memorial upon this location would have the further advantage that it need not be so high as to bring it into competition with the Washington Monument in order to make it visible from great distances, without danger of obstruction by buildings erected on private property. A monumental structure standing in a broad plain surrounded by an amphitheater of hills is as widely seen and is as impressive as one upon a hilltop. From the hills of the District and of Virginia the constantly recurring views of a great Lincoln Memorial, seen in association with the Washington Monument and the dome of the Capitol, would be impressive in the highest degree. ... As a matter of general design in relation to the plan of the city as a whole, any site upon the main east and west axis, in line with the Capitol and the Washington Monument, has an importance which no other site can claim; and the termination of that axis at the Potomac River gains a significance comparable only with that of the site selected in the plan of 1791 for the monument to Washington. The Lincoln Memorial would have its dignity enhanced by being so placed; and the termination of the axis by an object worthy of rank with the Washington Monument and the Capitol would be of the utmost value to the great composition."

The author of the commission's report concluded his case for the Potomac site by eloquently stating, "As I understand it, the place of honor is on the main axis of the plan. Lincoln, of all Americans next to Washington, deserves this place of honor. He was of the immortals. You must not approach too close to the immortals. His monument should stand alone, remote from the common habitations of man, apart from the business and turmoil of the city, isolated, distinguished, and serene. Of all the sites, this one, near the Potomac, is most suited to the purpose. In pursuance with your instructions we have considered carefully whether any location not specifically mentioned in your resolution meets the requirements. We are unable to find any such site. We, therefore, unanimously approve and recommend the Potomac Park site for the location of the Lincoln Memorial."

With these words ringing in their ears, the members of the committee approved the site on February 3, 1912.

Chapter 4: On Reclaimed Ground

"Owing to the fact that the Memorial was to be erected on reclaimed ground, the task of building strong foundations and constructing an edifice was an enormous one. Bids were called for and on February the twelfth, nineteen hundred and fourteen, contracts were awarded. The ground for the Memorial was broken without any ceremony and the actual construction was begun on March the twenty-seventh, only six weeks after the contracts were awarded." - James T. Matthews, author of *The Lincoln Memorial: An Athenian Temple in Memorial of a Great American* (1934)

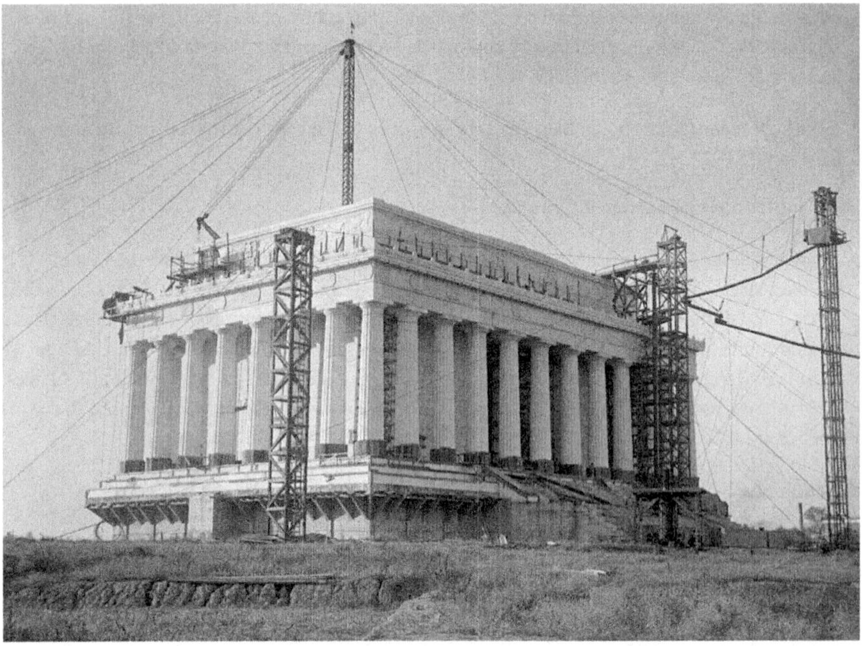

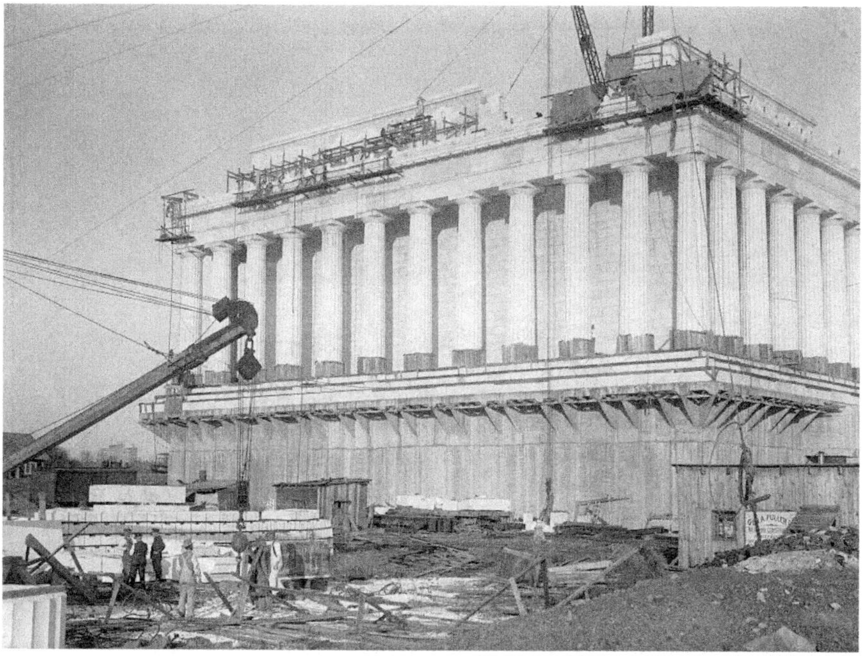

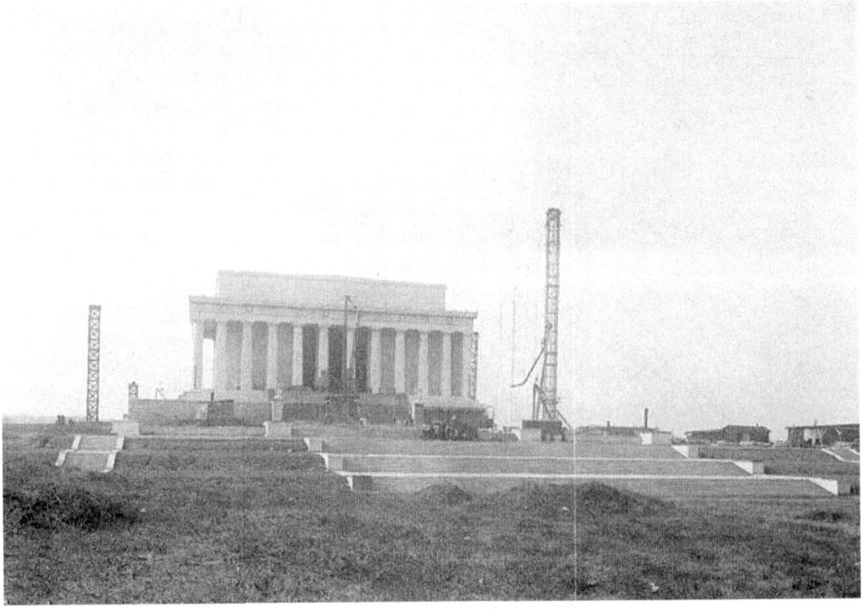

Pictures of the construction

Without question, the two men who most influenced the construction of the Lincoln Memorial were Henry Bacon, who designed the building, and Daniel French, who created the statue. According to an annual report made to Congress by the Memorial Committee in 1912, "On March 28 the Commission examined the new designs presented by the two architects…. Mr. Bacon submitted three designs, one being a slight modification of his original design and the other two being entirely new. … In a critical report on all the designs submitted, which had been requested of the Commission of Fine Arts…the recommendation was made that design A (the modified form of his first Potomac Park design), submitted by Mr. Bacon, be adopted, with such modifications as further study may suggest, and that Mr. Bacon be selected as the architect of the Memorial. On April 16 the Commission, by a majority vote, selected Mr. Henry Bacon as the architect to prepare the final design for the Lincoln Memorial to be submitted to the Commission for its decision, subject to the approval of Congress. Mr. Bacon at once proceeded with the preparation of this design, which was to embody certain modifications suggested to him as desirable, and submitted it to the Commission at a meeting held on July 3. The Commission, after a careful examination and discussion of the design presented by Mr. Bacon, has adopted it unanimously and recommends that Congress approve the construction of the Memorial upon the selected site in Potomac Park in accordance with the plans and designs of Mr. Bacon…subject to such minor modifications as may be determined upon by the architect in the preparation of the working drawings and approved by the Lincoln Memorial Commission."

Bacon

French

Of course, it is one thing to have a vision but something else altogether to see the vision to completion. One of the biggest concerns on Bacon's mind was the fact that the land around Potomac Park is notoriously wet due to its close proximity to the Potomac River, and though the height at which the Memorial was built should have solved this problem, Bacon was taking no chances. He later assured people, "The foundations of the Memorial and the work about it are carried down to solid rock, which was found to be from 44 to 65 feet below the original grade. Masonry approaches lead from the circular roadway, which surrounds a circular plateau 760 feet in diameter, to the steps ascending to the terrace supported by the granite retaining wall surrounding the Memorial. This wall is 256 feet 10 inches long, 187 feet wide, and 14 feet high. Above this rises the white marble Memorial, a structure of the Greek Doric order." In all, the foundation would be called upon to support more than 38,000 tons of granite and marble.

Once the groundbreaking ceremonies were over on February 12, 1914, the project moved along quickly, suffering few of the disasters that had plagued earlier construction projects in the District of Columbia. Major Douglas Weart, who worked on the project as a member of the Army Corps of Engineers, discussed parts of the process: "These foundations consist of two portions: (a) The portion below the original level of the park, known as the sub foundation* (b) the portion above this level, known as the upper foundation. The sub-foundation consists of 122 concrete piers formed in steel cylinders driven to bedrock. These cylinders vary in length from 49 to 65 feet and in diameter from 3 feet 6 inches to 4 feet 2 inches. They were sunk by being heavily weighted and water-jetted to a depth of absolute resistance. The earth was then removed by hand from each cylinder, the bedrock excavated to an additional depth of 2 feet, and the entire space filled with concrete, reinforced with twelve 1-inch square twisted bars set vertically in a circle 6 inches inside each cylinder. The tops of these cylinders at the ground level are splayed out to a rectangular shape (most of them square) and are connected by a grillage of reinforced concrete 1 foot thick. The upper foundation consists of concrete columns each about 45 feet in height erected upon the tops of these piers, being joined at their tops by arches poured integrally with them. Some of the columns are hollow and some are reinforced."

In addition to the two sections mentioned above, there were also a number of different sections for each different part of the Memorial. For instance, the terrace walls were built atop a slab foundation. According to Weart, "The beams supporting the deck slab were designed to act as struts between the top of the retaining wall and the building proper so as to prevent the wall from being thrown out of alignment due to the pressure of the earth fill against the wall. The ends of these struts were placed in slots in the wall of the main building without any rigid connection, so that they would move and adjust themselves to settlement of the terrace wall but would allow no movement of the top wall toward the building."

Within a year, the foundation was poured and dried. On Lincoln's birthday, February 12, 1915, a tall, flag festooned crane laid the Memorial's cornerstone in place. Concklin described the scene: "The corner stone of the Memorial was laid on Friday, February 12, 1915, at 3:07 p. m. The ceremonies observed were entirely informal. The stone used for the purpose is the base of the colonnade column at the northeast corner of the building, marked on the setting plans as No. AD 23. It is 7 feet 10 inches square by 2 feet 9 ½ inches high, with an additional 2 inches of height in the beginning of the column flutings integral with the base. The weight of this stone is slightly over 17 tons. In the center of the top of this stone a cavity was cut, 19 inches long, 14 inches wide, and 10 inches deep, the length being from east to west. In this opening were placed two copper boxes, specially designed by Mr. Frederick D. Owen, of the Office of Public Buildings and Public Parks…The contents of the box consisted of the following articles…The Bible, The Constitution of the United States, amended to May 1, 1913, Autograph of Lincoln (placed inside front cover of Bible)…Map of the United States, in two sections, 1914."

Conklin went on to provide a long list of items, including more maps and letters from those involved in the project. After the boxes were sealed, one inside the other, they were sealed inside the stone itself. As the corner stone was placed in position by the masons and declared by the Special Resident Commissioner to be set, he made the following statement as to the nature and purposes of the occasion: "The Lincoln Memorial Commission at its recent meeting determined that the laying of this corner stone should not be attended by any public function, as there was not time in which to prepare for such a gathering as would be commensurate with the occasion. The purpose of this Memorial that we are erecting is not to perpetuate the name or fame of him in whose honor it is [built], but is intended rather as an evidence to the generations that shall follow us of the admiration and love cherished by the American people. It can add no luster to the name and fame of Lincoln, but it is to stand through coming ages as evidence of the gratitude and devotion in which Lincoln is held by his countrymen. An American flag was then unfurled above the stone and the ceremonies concluded with the placing of mortar beneath the stone by the Special Resident Commissioner, the executive and disbursing officer, and others connected with the work."

Chapter 5: Two Reflection Pools

A picture of the reflecting pool on the National Mall

"The building stands on a terraced plateau which is one thousand feet in diameter at the base and seven hundred and fifty-five feet in diameter at the top where the building stands. The terrace has on the outer edge four rows of trees, separating the grounds of the Memorial from the grounds of Potomac Park and lending a pleasant landscape effect to the grounds. Between the Memorial and the Washington Monument are two reflection pools patterned after those of the Taj Mahal and reflecting both the Monument and the Memorial. The exterior of the building and the landscaping makes the Lincoln Memorial one of the most beautiful buildings of its kind in the world." - James T. Matthews, author of *The Lincoln Memorial: An Athenian Temple in Memorial of a Great American* (1934)

From the very beginning, Bacon was particularly enthusiastic about the project, especially because of its location. He later wrote, "Before beginning my study of the design for the Lincoln Memorial I believed that the site in Potomac Park was the best one and now that the Memorial is completed I am certain of it. Terminating the axis which unites it with the Washington Monument and the Capitol it has a significance which no other site can equal and any emulation or aspiration engendered by the Memorial to Lincoln and his great qualities is increased by the visual relation of the Memorial to the Washington Monument and the Capitol. Containing the National Legislature and judicial bodies, we have at one end of the axis a fine building, which is a monument to the United States Government. At the other end of the axis we now have a memorial to the man who saved that Government, and between the two is a monument to its founder. All three of these structures, stretching in one grand sweep from Capitol Hill to the Potomac River, will lend, one to the others, the associations and memories connected with each, and each will have thereby a heightened value."

Of course, the choice of location was no accident, and through careful planning, the Lincoln Memorial was able to complete Potomac Park, now known as the National Mall. Though there would be other smaller memorials and monuments added later, none would ever rival the magnificence of the Washington Monument, Congress, and Lincoln Memorial. As Bacon observed, "In a vista over 2 miles long these three large structures are so placed that they will testify forever to the reverence and honor which attended their erection, and the impression of their dignity and stateliness on the mind of the beholder will be augmented by their surroundings, for which there is a free field for symmetrical and proper arrangement. They are, however, sufficiently far apart for each to be distinguished, isolated, and serene, not conflicting in design or appearance the one with the others. ... The Memorial itself is free from the near approach of vehicles and traffic. Reverence and honor should suffer no distraction through lack of silence or repose in the presence of a structure reared to noble aims and great deeds." Although the growth Washington D.C. experienced during the 20th century may have given the lie to this ideal, the Lincoln Memorial still remains a place of reverent silence to this day.

Aerial view of the National Mall

Picture of the Lincoln Memorial from the Washington Monument

While Weart and Bacon were hard at work on the Memorial itself, another man, Irving Payne, was appointed by the Office of Public Buildings and Public Parks of the National Capital as the Memorial's Landscape Architect. He recalled, "During this year (1915), also about 150,000 cubic yards of material was dumped about the memorial as part of the fill required for the circular mound around the base of the building. This material was received without cost to the

Government. The architect completed the plans for the terrace wall and masonry approaches authorized in the urgent deficiency appropriation act approved February 28, 1916…"

Like the other two men, he had was devoted to making the most of the natural environment in which the memorial was set: "As seen from the great plaza fronting the entrance, the landscape architectural treatment is one whose elements have been successfully blended into a harmonious whole. The style of easy formality is characterized by a balance in the disposition of its foliage masses in relation to the main east and west axis of the Memorial, the net result of which is a landscape composition of unusual beauty and charm. The soft, rich green texture of the English and Japanese yews, combined with that of the various forms of quaint old-fashioned dwarf box, lend a particular feeling of distinction, solemnity, and repose. To the east of the Memorial, beginning at the foot of the steps leading from the entrance and extending toward the Washington Monument, lies the reflecting basin, in whose placid waters is reflected the Lincoln Memorial from the one end and from the other the stately reflection of the Washington Monument. Bordering each side of this monumental basin are two rows of stately English elms, an adequate embellishment of quiet dignity and innate charm."

The reflecting pool that he mentioned would soon become its own special part of the Potomac Park and would, over the next century, reflect not just the Lincoln Memorial but also the Washington Monument. More than that, though, it would reflect 100 years of change in the still young country, and in many ways it became a secondary symbol of the promises Lincoln gave his life to keep. According to Payne, "The pool was contemplated in the park plan of 1901. It was suggested because of the beauty and dignity of the waterways and canals in Versailles, France, and the reflecting basins at the Taj Mahal in India."

He then went on to describe the pool as it was being built at that time: "The pool consists of two basins, the larger of which is approximately 2,000 feet long by 160 feet wide, and the smaller 300 feet long by 160 feet wide. The maximum depth of the pools is 3 feet. The combined volume of the pools is 7,500,000 gallons, the smaller pool having 10 per cent of the total capacity. The supply and drainage systems are of sufficient capacity to fill or empty the pools in 24 hours. The coping of granite from Mount Airy, N. C., around the pools rests on a reinforced concrete T beam supported by piles at 20-foot intervals, which are driven to rock. The pools are waterproofed with a bituminous membrane protected on the aprons with concrete tile and on the bottoms with an asphalt mastic in the western section of the larger pool, and with roofing slate on the remainder of the surface. Display fountains are placed in the smaller pool and provision is made so that electric apparatus can be installed to operate colored lights for an electric fountain."

Unfortunately, Payne's work was not without its challenges, and many of them were out of his control. Concklin explained, "Work for the construction of the terrace wall and approaches was continued during this fiscal year but under difficulties incident to the World War which created a scarcity of labor and interruption of facilities for transporting materials to Washington. Severe winter weather also caused an unusual suspension of operations. ... Construction of the earth mound around the Memorial was continued. During the following fiscal year (1918-19) the erection of the terrace walls and approaches was continued and largely completed. Work was commenced grading for a gravel walk which was to be constructed on the terrace around the Memorial between the base of the building and the terrace wall."

With the Great War over, Bacon could begin work on the parts of the memorial that people would later come from all over the world to see. "The terrace wall was started at the south buttress of the main steps and built progressively around the Memorial to the north buttress. When work stopped in December, 1917, the wall and slab deck had been poured entirely on the east side and the wall about one-third completed on the south side. During November and December, 1917, the back fill was made on this portion of the wall. ... The deck slab was poured at the southwest corner in June, 1918, and up to September 1, 1918.... When the back fill was made at this corner the settlement became much more rapid, so that by November 8, 1918, it had reached a total of 0.59 foot. During this settlement the wall maintained its alignment, and the horizontal joints of the granite were not affected. Similar conditions to the above held true during the remainder of the construction."

Although the settling was not initially worrisome, it became more of a concern as time went on. By 1920, Weart and the others in charge determined "it would not be safe to permit the settlement to go on indefinitely." He wrote, "As there was no indication that the settlement would stop in the near future, it was decided to underpin the foundation. The scheme for underpinning contemplated sinking steel cylinders between the columns supporting the wall and the deck to bedrock, filling the same with concrete and carrying the load by means of transverse steel beams resting on the column and carried in under the foundation footings. Before work was commenced, however, the scheme was changed to provide for concrete columns being placed directly under the piers supporting the wall and terrace, thus eliminating the beams. The foundations of the approaches were to be supported on a system of steel girders, resting on concrete piers carried to bedrock, with steel needle beams through the columns."

Chapter 6: One of the Most Beautiful in Washington

"Approaching the Lincoln Memorial, one is reminded of the ancient temples of Athens. The colonnades bear out this impression and mark the building as one of the most beautiful in Washington. The exterior represents the union of the states, the frieze above the colonnades bearing the names of the thirty-six states of the Union at the time of Mr. Lincoln and the walls above bearing the names of the forty-eight states existing today. The structure is of the Greek Doric order and is built of the finest quarried marble." - James T. Matthews, the author of *The Lincoln Memorial: An Athenian Temple in Memorial of a Great American* (1934)

After the foundation was laid, work on the memorial moved along rapidly. Concklin wrote, "Work upon the superstructure was begun on February 10, 1915, by the contractors for that portion of the work who on that date set the first stone of the exterior, and by June 30 of that year there had been completed the three step courses surrounding the building, the fill under the colonnade floor and portions of that floor, the wall ashlar and parts of some of the colonnade columns and the exterior walls on an average about half of their height to the cornice. During the next fiscal year, ending June 30, 1916, the exterior walls of the building, the colonnade floor, the columns and the main cornice were practically completed and portions of the attic story placed. ... During the year from July 1, 1915, to June 30, 1917, all of the exterior marble and the interior marble and limestone work were completed, the attic story finished, the copper roof constructed and progress made on the heating and plumbing equipment. Based upon proposals received July 26, 1916, a contract was entered into on September 15, 1916, for constructing the terrace wall and masonry approaches. Work under this was commenced at once and by the end of the fiscal year considerable work had been done in the way of concrete foundation, concrete wall and slab, and laying cast-iron drain pipe. The work of constructing the earth mound around the Memorial progressed throughout the year with material received and deposited without cost to the United States. During this year a contract was entered into, on October 24, 1916, for the interior decorations and wall painting. The entire superstructure of the building was completed on October 26, 1917, and taken over by representatives of the Government."

One thing that immediately strikes a visitor to the memorial is the sheer size of the building itself, and this is as Bacon planned it. He listed its specifications: "The colonnade is 188 feet 4 inches long and 118 feet 6 inches wide, resting on a platform composed of three steps, 8 feet high in all, the bottom step of which is 201 feet 10 inches long and 132 feet wide. There are 38 columns in the colonnade, including the two which stand in the entrance. They are 44 feet high, 7 feet 5 inches in diameter at the base, and are composed of 11 drums each, excluding the cap. ... The height of the building from the top of the foundation just below the main floor to the top of the attic is 79 feet 10 inches. The height above grade from the foot of the terrace walls is 99 feet. The total height from the bottom of the foundations, which rest on bedrock, varies from 169 to 192 feet. The two tripods on the two buttresses flanking the steps leading up to the entrance to the building are 11 feet high, and each is cut from a single block of pink Tennessee marble."

The colonnade was completed in 1917, allowing for other portions of the Memorial to be added. According to Concklin, the most prominent decorations "consist of the names of the 36 States in the Union at the time of Lincoln's death and of the 48 States which composed the Union when the Memorial was dedicated on May 30, 1922. The first are carved on the frieze above the colonnade, each separated from the other by a medallion composed of a double wreath of leaves, while the cornice above is decorated with a carved scroll interspersed at regular intervals with a projecting lion's head. On the attic walls above the colonnade are carved the names of the 48 States which compose the Union to-day above which appears a continuous string of garlands supported by the wings of elaborately carved eagles, the end of each garland being affixed to the wall with a ribbon having flowing ends at the top of which are two palm leaves. Under the name of each State in both courses is shown in Roman numerals the date of its admission into the

Union."

Detail of the bas-relief frieze on the memorial

Next came the massive roof, elegantly carved with elaborate festoons, eagles and wreaths by local sculptor Ernest C. Bairstow. It was put in place by some of the largest cranes available at that time.

One of the things that made the project move along at such a rapid pace was that Congress continued to support the work with appropriations. The second decade of the 20th century was a very prosperous time for the country, so there were fewer spending constraints. Following the first $50,000 earmarked for the project in 1911, Congress approved another $300,000 for construction costs in 1913. From there, the legislature consistently set aside money for the memorial throughout its completion, including $400,000 in 1914, $600,000 in 1915, $963,000 in 1916, and $331,000 in 1917, bringing the total spent on construction to $2,594,000. This sum was supplemented in 1921 with another $345,720 "for additional work on the masonry approaches and terrace around the Lincoln Memorial, including foundations to rock and all necessary expenses of every kind incident thereto."

The entire cost of the project was nearly $3 million for the building itself, but there were other things to spend money on as well. Concklin noted, "In addition to the appropriations made for the Memorial building, its terrace wall, and approaches, Congress provided the sum of $100,000 in sundry civil act approved March 4, 1921, for constructing roads and walks surrounding the

Memorial and roads and walks leading thereto from existing improved roads, to be expended by the Lincoln Memorial Commission. Also $5,000 for expenses of dedicating the Memorial, this having been originally appropriated in the sundry civil act approved July 19, 1919, re-appropriated by sundry civil act approved June 5, 1920, and again re-appropriated by sundry civil act approved March 4, 1921. A total sum of $584,000 was appropriated for the reflecting pools east of the Memorial, the amount being granted in four installments of $175,000, $84,000, $250,000, and $75,000 by sundry civil acts approved July 19, 1919, June 5, 1920, and March 4, 1921, and War Department act approved June 30, 1922. These funds were expended by the Officer in Charge of Public Buildings and Grounds, under whose direction the pools were constructed."

Chapter 7: Three Chambers

"The interior of the building is divided into three chambers by Greek Ionic columns fifty feet high and five or six feet in diameter. The center chamber, which one enters after mounting the steps leading to the entrance of the Memorial, is the largest and the most impressive of the three chambers. Directly facing the doorway is the statue by Daniel French and the visitor cannot but marvel at it." - James T. Matthews, the author of *The Lincoln Memorial: An Athenian Temple in Memorial of a Great American* (1934)

With the exterior completed, next came work on the inner chamber, known in design circles as the cella. By this time, the decision had been reached to make the statue of Lincoln significantly larger than originally planned, so adjustments had to be made to accommodate the larger statue. Concklin explained, "The reconstruction of the platform for the pedestal and statue and of the panel behind it in the west wall of the interior was continued. Additional steel beams were placed beneath this platform to support the increased weight resulting from the enlargement of the statue and pedestal. The setting of the stones for the revised panel was finished. There was also completed and placed in position at the tops of the north and south interior walls the decorative paintings which portray in allegorical form the principles expressed in the Gettysburg Speech and Mr. Lincoln's Second Inaugural Address which are, respectively, carved on the tablets beneath the paintings."

Gregory F. Maxwell's picture of the Second Inaugural Address inscribed on the memorial

Gregory F. Maxwell's picture of the Gettysburg Address inscription

The interior was completed in the spring of 1916, after which came the 38 columns, one representing each of the 36 states making up the United States when Lincoln took office and two more to flank the entrance. This is when things got interesting, at least for Bacon: "There are some architectural refinements in the work not common in modern buildings. The columns are not vertical, being slightly tilted inward toward the building, the four corner columns being tilted more than the others. The outside face of the entablature is also inclined inward, but slightly less than the columns underneath it. The wall of the Memorial Hall inclines inward least of all. The marble of the exterior was quarried at the Colorado-Yule marble quarries in the Rocky Mountains in Colorado 10,000 feet above sea level, and about 300 miles west of Denver. Some of the stones are of unusual size, weighing 23 tons each."

Close up picture of the columns

The fluted columns served not only to hold up the roof of the structure but also to divide it into different areas of interest, thereby preventing the visitor from becoming overwhelmed by the space while at the same time preserving the awe Bacon wanted people to feel. He continued, "The interior of the building is divided into three chambers by Greek Ionic columns 50 feet high and 5 feet 6 inches diameter at the base. The central chamber contains the statue, and the two side chambers contain the memorial speeches. The walls of these chambers are Indiana limestone, and the ceiling, which is 60 feet above the finished floor, is designed with bronze girders ornamented with laurel and pine leaves. The marble panels between the girders are of Alabama marble saturated with melted beeswax to make them translucent. The interior floor, which is 2 inches thick, and the wall base are of pink Tennessee marble." These details were important to his readers, as they reminded everybody of the contributions of both Northern and Southern states to Lincoln's memorial.

Though the statue of Lincoln is no doubt the most memorable feature of the memorial, there are a number of other impressive (though less well known) interior designs, including two large murals painted by the popular French artist Jules Guerin. Topping the north and south walls, they impress the viewer not just with their beauty but also with their colossal size, each being 12 feet tall and 60 feet wide. Concklin specifically pointed out that the murals "were painted by the artist without assistance. Adopting his description they typify in allegory the principles evident in the life of Abraham Lincoln. There are six groups in an Enchanted Grove, each group having for a background cypress trees, the emblem of Eternity."

On the south wall, above a copy of the Gettysburg Address carved in huge letters, there are three painted groups. Concklin described each, beginning with Freedom and Liberty: "The Angel of Truth is giving Freedom and Liberty to the Slave. The shackles of bondage are falling from the arms and feet. They are guarded by two sibyls." Next came Justice and the Law, the "central figure in the Chair of the Law has the Sword of Justice in one hand; with the other she holds the Scroll of the Law; seated at her feet are two sibyls, interpreting the Law. The standing figures on each side are the Guardians of the Law, holding the torches of Intelligence." Finally, there is Immortality: "The central figure is being crowned with the Laurel Wreath of Immortality. The standing figures are Faith, Hope, and Charity. On each side is the Vessel of Wine and the Vessel of Oil, the symbols of Everlasting Life."

The North Wall features an inscription of Lincoln's Second Inaugural Address in similarly large letters. Above it is the second mural, also featuring three painted groups, the first being Unity. Concklin described Unity: "The Angel of Truth is joining the hands of the laurel-crowned figures of the North and South, signifying Unity, and with her protecting wings ennobles the arts of Painting, Philosophy, Music, Architecture, Chemistry, Literature, and Sculpture. Immediately behind the figure of Music is the veiled figure of the Future." Unity in turn is joined by Fraternity; "The central figure of Fraternity holds together with her encircling arms the Man and the Woman, the symbols of the Family developing the abundance of the Earth. On each side is the Vessel of Wine and the Vessel of Oil, the symbols of Everlasting Life." Finally, there is Charity, "attended by her handmaidens…giving the Water of Life to the Halt and the Blind and caring for the Orphans."

Concklin concluded his description of the paintings by noting, "The decorations are painted on canvas, each piece of which weighed 600 pounds. About 300 pounds of paint were used. There are 48 figures in the two panels, the standing figures being 8 feet high. Almost as many models were used as there are figures. The canvas is affixed to the wall with a mixture of white lead and Venetian varnish. The decorations are absolutely weatherproof, the paint being mixed with white wax and kerosene. The wax hardens but does not allow the paint to crack. Chemically the wax is similar to that found in the tombs of the Kings of Egypt, which is said to be still pliable. The ornamentation on the bronze ceiling beams, consisting of laurel and pine leaves, was also executed by Mr. Guerin."

Chapter 8: Its Great Beauty

"It was decided that the real memorial to Lincoln should be a statue of the man himself. After careful consideration of a number of sculptors and their work, the Commission decided upon Mr. Daniel French to execute the colossal statue planned for the interior of the building. ... The statue is nineteen feet high and also nineteen feet in width at the point of greatest width. Mr. Lincoln is represented as seated, his arms resting on the arms of the chair and his hands clasping the ends of the chair arms. The naturalness of the posture and the variety of emotions which the sculptor has portrayed in the face of the statue, make one wonder at its realness. Almost all of the elements of the great character are portrayed, strength, mental power, sympathy, kindliness, humor, and determination being shown in the features. The head is slightly bent as though Mr. Lincoln were musing and he sits facing the Capitol of the country he loved and served. One has to study the statue from all angles to appreciate fully its great beauty and to realize the remarkable qualities which Mr. French has portrayed so accurately in his work." - James T. Matthews, the author of *The Lincoln Memorial: An Athenian Temple in Memorial of a Great American* (1934)

Naturally, the centerpiece of the Lincoln Memorial is the colossal statue of Lincoln himself, so it should come as no surprise that the committee took great pains to choose the right sculptor for this all important feature. Ultimately, the committee chose Daniel Chester French. According to one article that ran at that time, "French has been commissioned to execute the portrait statue of Lincoln which is to be permanently placed in the Lincoln Memorial at Washington, now under construction. The fact that Mr. French was a member of the Federal Commission of Fine Arts might have seemed to have prohibited his undertaking this important work, but the truth is that Mr. French's term of service expires in the early part of 1915 and therefore this was not an obstacle. Mr. French is without question one of the foremost sculptors of our day. His Milmore Memorial, 'Death Staying the Hand of the Young Sculptor,' his 'Gallaudet Group,' and his 'Alma Mater' are among the finest works of the kind which have been produced in modern times. Furthermore, Mr. French and Mr. Bacon, the architect of the Lincoln Memorial, have for some years worked together, the latter designing the architectural setting for many of the sculptor's more recent works. The selection of Mr. French as the sculptor of this Lincoln statue would, therefore, seem peculiarly fortunate and proper."

In spite of his initial enthusiasm, French soon learned that he had a bigger job on his hands than he originally planned. According to Concklin, "A contract was entered into with the sculptor on December 31, 1917, for increasing the size of the statue from about 10 feet in height to about 19 feet or, including the plinth, 20 feet, which was necessitated by the fact that experiments in the building with models had demonstrated that the statue as originally designed would be too small for the prominent position it would occupy as the principal feature of the Memorial. This enlargement of the statue required an increase in the size and a change in the design of the panel in the limestone wall in front of which the statue was to be placed, and a contract for this was entered into on December 24, 1917, with the builders of the superstructure."

French began working on the statue in his New York studio and had much of it completed before he shipped it to Washington in late 1919. At that time, it, along with its pedestal, was made up of 19 separate stones which he then carved in place atop their Tennessee marble pedestal before having "the statue trimmed, cleaned, and pointed up." According to the Smithsonian American Art Museum, "The nineteen-foot statue was carved from French's seven-foot plaster model by the Piccirilli Brothers who used twenty-eight identical blocks of Georgia marble. It took four years, and when the carving was completed the twenty-eight pieces were brought to Washington and assembled on site. The Piccirilli Brothers also carved the two urns in front of the statue of Lincoln. Ernest C. Bairstow did the stonework on the memorial. Evelyn Beatrice Longman modeled the eagles and double wreaths for the decorative wall panels near the carved words of Lincoln's addresses, as a favor to French and Bacon when their funding to complete the work ran short. The inscription on the wall behind Lincoln reads: IN THIS TEMPLE, AS IN THE HEARTS OF THE PEOPLE, FOR WHOM HE SAVED THE UNION, THE MEMORY OF ABRAHAM LINCOLN IS ENSHRINED FOREVER."

Picture of the statue being worked on

    Shortly after its completion, Matthews wrote, "The chamber in which this magnificent statue rests, is sixty feet wide and seventy-four feet in depth, while the two small chambers at each end are sixty-three feet wide and thirty-eight feet deep. On the wall at the end of the chamber to the right is engraved the Second Inaugural Address while on the end wall of the chamber to the left is engraved the Gettysburg Address. Above these two Addresses are mural paintings typifying the principles which guided Mr. Lincoln, freedom and liberty, justice and law, immortality, unity, fraternity, and charity. These paintings are the unassisted work of Jules Guerin and are of such beauty that they cannot fail to catch the eye and captivate the emotions. The silent halls of the Lincoln Memorial create a quiet atmosphere of reverence which impress all visitors and make the Memorial truly a shrine to the memory of Mr. Lincoln. Every detail of the building, both of the interior and of the exterior, portray dignity and beauty, and make the building a real temple in honor of the great American. It is true that Mr. Lincoln is enshrined in the hearts of countless fellow Americans but until they have visited the Lincoln Memorial, have seen the beauty of the building, and have marveled at the statue and studied it until they have taken in every detail, they cannot appreciate fully the majestic Memorial which a grateful people have erected, nor the influence which this man exercised that could reach across time and grasp the heartstrings of all who visit his shrine. It well may be said that the Lincoln Memorial is a beautiful tribute to the greatest American of recent times."

    Returning to the structure itself, Bacon shared the belief that the memorial should unite the nation and honor all states: "The exterior of the Memorial symbolizes the Union of the United States of America. Surrounding the walls of the Memorial Hall is a colonnade of the States of the Union, the frieze above it bearing the names of the 36 States existing at the time of Lincoln's death. On the walls above the colonnade are inscribed the names of the 48 States existing today. These walls and columns enclose the sanctuary containing three memorials to Abraham Lincoln. In the place of honor is found a colossal marble statue of the man himself, facing the Washington Monument and the Capitol. On the end wall to the right of the central space where the statue is placed, and separated from it by a row of columns, is the monument of the Second Inaugural Address. On the similar wall at the opposite end of the hall is the monument of the Gettysburg Speech."

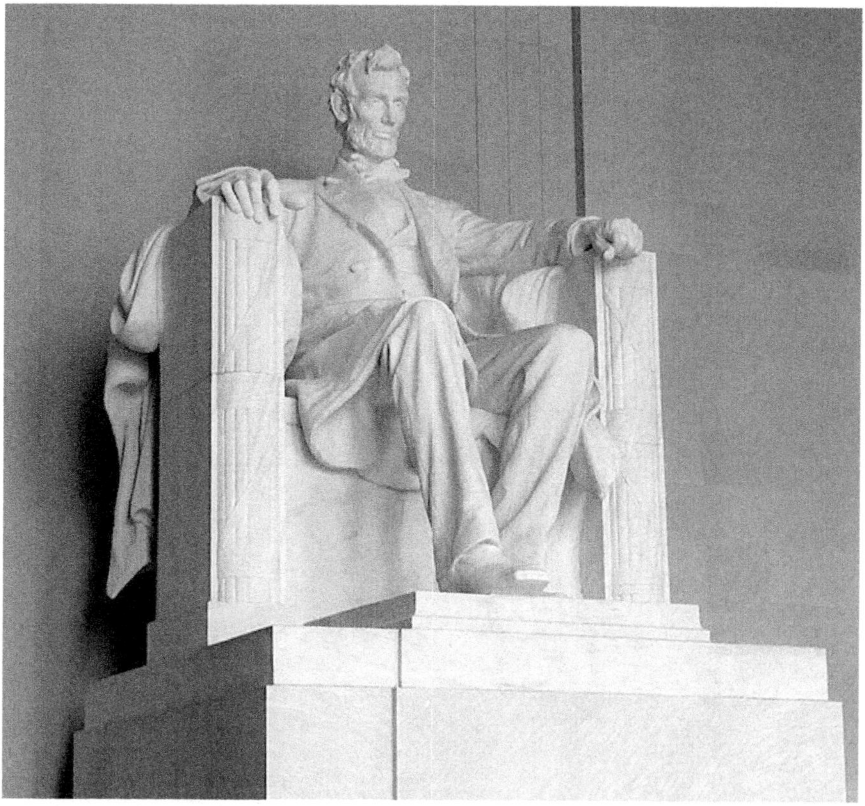

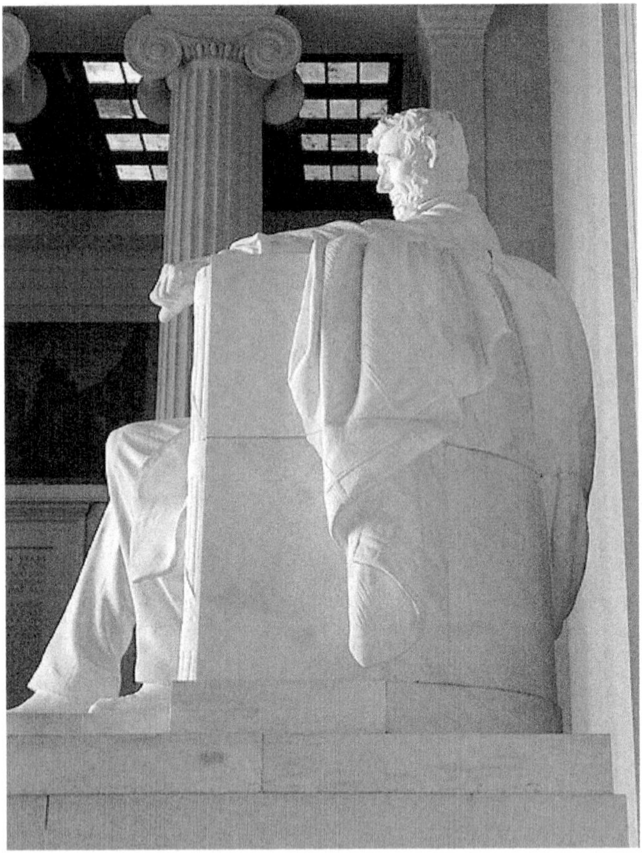

Pictures of the completed statue

Chapter 9: The Dedication of the Building

"Eleven years after the creation of the Lincoln Memorial Commission, the Lincoln Memorial was completed. May the thirteenth, nineteen hundred and twenty-two, was set as the date for the dedication of the building and its presentation by the Commission to the United States government. An elaborate ceremony was planned with speeches by government officials and a flag ceremony by the veterans of the Union Army. Amplifiers were installed in order that the large number of spectators expected to witness the dedication might hear the program. Fifty thousand persons were present for the ceremony, at which Chairman Taft presided, and a number of Civil War veterans were in attendance also." - James T. Matthews, the author of *The Lincoln Memorial: An Athenian Temple in Memorial of a Great American* (1934)

Picture of President Harding at the dedication

After the statue was finished, there were only a few final details to be completed. Concklin later recalled, "Work upon the earth mound was continued. The construction of the approaches to the building, the terrace wall, and the walk on the terrace were all finished during this fiscal year. This left only the painting of the bronze ceiling beams and the introduction of electric lights, both of which were completed during the next fiscal year ending June 30, 1921. The work of constructing the earth mound around the Memorial was practically completed during this year. The mound contains about 500,000 cubic yards of earth filling, all of which was received without expense to the United States. During this year, also under a special appropriation made by Congress for the purpose, there were constructed a bituminous macadam circular roadway around the Memorial with a concrete sidewalk bordering its inner edge, a similar roadway with concrete sidewalk on either side on the line of Twenty-third Street leading in to the circular roadway from B Street and a third roadway of similar construction and with concrete sidewalk on either side running between Twenty- first and Twenty-second Streets out from the main circular roadway to B Street."

Since the project had taken nearly a decade to complete, by the time the final touches were put on the statue, the work that had been done earlier was in need of repair. Concklin noted, "During the fiscal year ending June 30, 1922, the terrace wall and approaches which had been showing signs of settlement were underpinned by supporting their existing foundations on concrete piers carried to bedrock. Repairs were also made to the terrace wall and approaches where they had been cracked and damaged by settlement. This work was done with a special appropriation made by Congress at the request of the Lincoln Memorial Commission. This completed the Memorial and its surroundings. The grounds around the Memorial were graded, seeded, and planted with trees and shrubs by the office which is in charge of the park. It also completed, during the fiscal year ended June 30, 1923, a reflecting pool extending from a point about 450 feet east of the Memorial out toward Seventeenth Street. This pool is 2,027 feet long and 160 feet wide, in which the Memorial is reflected as in a mirror. Between the east end of this pool and Seventeenth Street a transverse pool was constructed, 291 feet long and 160 feet wide."

Fortunately, all the repairs were safely completed by May 30, 1922, and on that day, people gathered from all over the country to pay homage to Lincoln and the other men who had worked so faithfully to honor him. According to Matthews, the dedication began on a reverent note. "The invocation was offered by Dr. Radcliffe, pastor-emeritus of the New York Avenue Presbyterian Church of Washington where Mr. Lincoln worshipped during his term of office as President and where he sought spiritual aid when discouraged by the tide of events which seemed destined to overthrow the nation. Mr. Edwin Markham, acclaimed by many as the American Poet-Laureate, read a copy of his famous poem "Lincoln, the Man of the People" which he had especially revised for the occasion."

Still, in Matthews' mind at least, it was not words but actions that spoke most eloquently that day: "Perhaps the most impressive part of the ceremony was the flag ceremony in which a thin line of blue-clad Union veterans who had served with Mr. Lincoln as their Commander-in-Chief, participated. To them the Memorial meant more than to any one of the fifty thousand spectators since they had loved and followed the man to whose honor the building was erected."

Indeed, Major General Thomas Pilcher, the Commander of the Grand Army of the Republic at the time, spoke eloquently himself at the event: "In the name of my comrades of the Grand Army of the Republic representing all who answered Lincoln's call to arms, all who fought valiantly on land and sea for four years for the country's very life; representing the 400,000 who died in the line of duty that the Nation might live, and the million and a half who have died since, I accept this high honor. The greatest leaders in that bloody struggle are now no more; their memory remains; that for which they strove abides; the magnitude of the issues for which they gave their devotion looms continually larger as the years multiply. It is the highest pride of my comrades that they fought with exalted courage, endured with patient persistence, and died bravely when need be to make real Lincoln's ideals. They admired and loved him as a man, revered him as a patriot, and idolized him as their leader. This great Memorial is the crowning glory of the lives of Lincoln's soldiers, sailors, and marines, who still survive and today join in this magnificent tribute to their illustrious chief, whose life and words have been their inspiration."

Next, the dedication took a surprisingly progressive turn, especially in the still segregated city.

According to Matthews, "Because of the action of Mr. Lincoln in abolishing slavery and giving the opportunities of citizenship to countless colored people, Professor Robert R. Moton, a teacher at the most famous of colored schools, Tuskegee Institute, was asked to make a short address in keeping with the spirit of the ceremony. This he did and in a remarkably beautiful speech extolled the virtues of the martyred leader."

Following Moton's words, poet Edwin Markham rose to read a poem he had composed for the event. Entitled "LINCOLN, THE MAN OF THE PEOPLE," it concluded:

> "He held the ridgepole up, and spike again
>
> The rafters of the Home. He held his place--
>
> Held the long purpose like a growing tree--
>
> Held on through blame and faltered not at praise.
>
> And when he fell in whirlwind, he went down
>
> As when a lordly cedar, green with boughs.
>
> Goes down with a great shout upon the hills,
>
> And leaves a lonesome place against the sky."

The day was a particularly joyful one for Taft, who had by this time lost much of his political favor, as well as his once much cherished friendship with Teddy Roosevelt. "Chairman Taft made a speech of presentation for the Lincoln Memorial Commission and President Harding, in the main address of the day, accepted the gift for the government, praising the work of the Commission and all those engaged in the construction of the Memorial, and setting forth the high character of the Emancipator. Ex-President Woodrow Wilson had been requested by the Commission to participate in the Dedication Ceremony but was unable to do so on account of illness. He sent a note commending the Commission upon the accomplishment of the great task entrusted to it."

Taft was followed by the sitting President, Warren G. Harding, who called Lincoln a "superman" and observed, "Like the great Washington, whose monumental shaft towers nearby as a fit companion to the Memorial we dedicate today, the two testifying the grateful love of all Americans to founder and savior; like Washington, Lincoln was a very natural human being, with the frailties mixed with the virtues of humanity. There are neither supermen nor demigods in the government of kingdoms, empires, or republics. It will be better for our conception of government and its institutions if we will understand this fact. It is vastly greater than finding the superman if we justify the confidence that our institutions are capable of bringing into authority, in time of stress, men big enough and strong enough to meet all demands."

No dedication then or now is complete without appropriate music, and there was plenty at this event. According to Matthews, "At intervals throughout the program the United States Marine Band rendered patriotic selections in keeping with the ceremony. The entire ceremony was appropriate and inspiring and it was with a sense of satisfaction that millions of Americans realized that Abraham Lincoln had at last received the homage and honor his brilliant service deserved."

Erich Weber's picture of the Lincoln Memorial at dusk

A picture from the Lincoln Memorial taken during the 1963 March on Washington

Aerial view of the Lincoln Memorial

Bibliography

Concklin, Edward. *The Lincoln Memorial Washington.* (1927)

Hufbauer, Benjamin. *Presidential Temples: How Memorials and Libraries Shape Public Memory* (2006)

Matthews, James. *The Lincoln Memorial: An Athenian Temple in Memory of a Great American* (1934)

Thomas, Christopher A. *The Lincoln Memorial and American Life* (2002)

The Jefferson Memorial

Chapter 1: Early Washington

Although the monument was a 20th century creation, the seeds of the Jefferson Memorial's creation lie far back in time and date back to the gradual cultural and political evolution that occurred after the nation's founding in the late 18th century. At that time, and in the succeeding decades, Washington D.C. was a most unimposing city, described as either quaintly rural or appallingly squalid depending on the commentator's predispositions. Even the most favorable observers noted that the future metropolis appeared as a cluster of barely-connected villages, and what eventually became the National Mall was then an area of vegetable gardens and refuse heaps. The British burning of Washington during the War of 1812 served to depress the fortunes of the national capital further.

From the city's earliest days, plans had been afoot to place at least some monuments in Washington, and naturally, the most prominent of these plans called for a statue honoring the eponymous statesman and general George Washington. However, this grandiose project, which envisioned a remarkable equestrian statue of the country's first president, never actually materialized; though it was apparently sincerely and seriously desired, there was never enough money to erect the statue in the new nation's capital.

Just two decades before the American Civil War erupted over the long-simmering question of slavery, which had lurked in the background of America's political system from the moment of the Declaration of Independence, a famous English writer and traveler had essentially written off the city on the Potomac as ever amounting to anything. "Charles Dickens, visiting from England in 1842, saw the city as a ruin in the making: 'a monument to a deceased project, with not even a legible inscription to record its departed greatness.' A few decades after its inception, the capital was fast becoming a memorial to its own failure." (Savage, 2009, 26).

Nonetheless, there were signs that Washington's seeming slide into mediocrity was not destined to continue forever. Elegant buildings were being erected elsewhere in the United States, frequently following the Neoclassical tradition, and if anything, American architects were largely responsible for reviving classicism in architecture during the late 18th and early 19th centuries, simultaneously giving it a facelift for their era. With building projects taking place across the United States, including Thomas Jefferson's famous estate of Monticello (whose design ultimately provided partial inspiration for the Jefferson Memorial), it was only a matter of time until new structures appeared along the Potomac as well.

Martin Falbisoner's picture of Monticello

Fiske Kimball, a prominent 20th century American historian and architect who served as the Restoration Committee Chairman of the Thomas Jefferson Memorial Foundation during the years leading up to and immediately following the memorial's construction, extensively studied the role of Americans in developing the Neoclassical movement. It was his discovery that Neoclassical architecture found its main initial impetus in the New World that prompted him to support the use of this design style in the Memorial building: "The classical revival was indeed a movement which had its beginnings abroad, and which there also had the same ultimate ideal, the temple. By priority in embodiment of this ideal, however, and by greater literalness and universality in its realization, America reveals an independent initiative. […] [The] Virginia Capitol, designed in 1785, preceded the […] first of the great European temple reproductions […] by twenty-two years." (Kimball, 1922, 146).

For a generation or two after the Revolution, the United States remained quite provincial, a spacious and pleasant (for its free inhabitants at least) agrarian backwater but a backwater nonetheless. During this time, it was perhaps unsurprising that Washington D.C. remained largely undeveloped relative to the mighty capitals of the European nations, which had been centers for government, commerce, culture, and art for several centuries and in some cases thousands of years. The federal government was also relatively weak at this time, though it was already recognized by the Founding Fathers that this could be a recipe for disaster if permitted to continue.

During the early 19th century, however, the winds of change were blowing ever more powerfully. The Industrial Revolution was gradually developing, and the United States, with its large number of entrepreneurs, its vigorously industrious free population, and its vast resources of space, mineral wealth, water, and agricultural land, was well-positioned to exploit this emergent technological revolution. Westward expansion brought with it both gigantic untapped reserves of metals, land, and timber, as well as a dynamic, driving spirit and a sense of unlimited possibilities absent from the fully defined nations of the Old World, known for their hard-cut boundaries and rigid social structures.

The Civil War also drastically changed the United States and its formerly-languishing capital. In order to be victorious in the Civil War, the federal government transformed itself from the sleepy center of a breakaway agrarian British province into the powerful capital of an independent nation. Furthermore, with the Union threatened, American patriots in the North wanted a location that more explicitly symbolized and confirmed the collective strength and cohesion of the United States. In turn, the Civil War greatly accelerated America's growth in several ways. Meeting the need for muskets, rifles, artillery, troop trains, ironclad warships, and all the other paraphernalia of organized violence provided a huge boost to the development of the country's industrial capacity.

It was no accident that it was precisely during this period that an 11-year project to create a new dome on the Capitol was undertaken. Soaring to 288 feet, comprised of nearly 4,500 tons of cast iron, and topped by the 20-foot tall bronze Statue of Freedom (originally entitled "Freedom Triumphant in War and Peace"), the Capitol's dome represented the determination of many Americans to maintain the Union. It was also an important step in launching a series of renovations and monuments across Washington that transformed the Potomac township into a fully realized capital city. Subsequent additions to Washington were reaffirmations of American identity and the overall solidarity of the republic, and American economic growth supplied the money and resources necessary to fill the capital with striking emblems and architectural expressions of national identity.

The Capitol under construction in 1861 at the time of Lincoln's inauguration

As a result, the old, quiet, slightly shabby Washington D.C. ended with the Civil War. From that moment forward, the development of the capital's monuments and landmarks was self-conscious and deliberate, an expression of patriotism that established a number of powerful symbols to reinforce the unity of all Americans and the country's bedrock foundation of personal freedom. The Jefferson Monument was a late addition but would come to be one of the most poignant emblems of this new Washington.

Chapter 2: Planning the Jefferson Memorial

Washington D.C. began to embody American ideals through symbolic representations from the start. However, the true period of monumental development occurred following the Civil War and through the mid-20th century. These constructions were often the subjects of bitter disputes and last-minute changes of plan, but a uniquely American monumental structure was nevertheless created during this three-quarter century interval.

Most European capitals made use of symbols that dominated with colossal, immovable grandeur, expressing the iron strength of dynasties and empires, but American designers and architects took a rather different approach. The United States' version was to make far more use of space and a sort of "connect the dots" approach wherein each monument was to serve as the jumping-off point for seeking out the next. In this way, the collection of monuments could be more of a journey than a decisive endpoint, and the concept of space and dynamism was itself a message of the cultural character which the new Washington sought to symbolize: "By grouping the assemblage of grounds into a "great space" the [plan] was making an important move. The term great space now referred not only to the size of the land area, as it would have for Downing, but also to a more significant qualitative dimension. Space itself now had an integrative power, knitting together various spots and structures into a compelling whole." (Savage, 2009, 160).

Thus, the physical vastness of America and the possibilities opened up by freedom and modernity were not something that divided the nation but the element that united it. The monuments were to be links in a chain that extended in all directions, with none of them representing a culmination or ending point. Of course, the Jefferson Memorial is one of the focal points of the chain of monuments around it, but it also incorporated this idea into its actual structure, though most visitors to the site do not realize the symbolism inherent in the design. It is open on all sides and enables the viewer to gaze through its walls to the prospect beyond, a feature that serves a deliberate statement that even the mighty framer of the Declaration of Independence is not an answer but the springboard for new questions.

The Washington Monument was one of the earliest monuments to an individual that was begun after the Civil War, but it required many years to complete. Many critics directed torrents of hatred at the plain, narrow, towering obelisk, instead suggesting elaborate stone confections bristling with allegorical figures and festooned with bas reliefs. Undeterred, Thomas L. Casey, the final architect, remained determined to make the Washington Monument as he saw it, and the struggle over the monument's final form would end up being similar to the histrionic squabbling involved in the planning of the Jefferson Memorial a few decades later. Casey wanted a plain monument which was an expression of space and achievement rather than a grandiloquent pageant in stone. His plan called for the first steam-operated elevator inside the shaft and a high observation platform from which the whole vista of Washington D.C. could be surveyed. Above all, he wanted to make something remarkable, and a monument that symbolized achievement by itself being an achievement. As Savage points out, the Washington Monument was designed "to be a technological marvel. The Joint Commission had directed him to design for 525 feet, and he decided to make the most of it by including the highest passenger elevator as well, lit within by electric lights. '525 feet is higher than any structure yet erected by the hand of man,' he wrote his father in 1878, 'and such a height is hardly appreciated by even intelligent persons.'" (Savage, 2009, 124).

The architect's proposed design met with a storm of opposition, championed by the rich and powerful aesthete William J. Corcoran, who also led the commission tasked with determining the final form of the monument. Ultimately, Casey defeated Corcoran through bulldog tenacity, holding onto his goal until the rest of those involved in the decision grew so exasperated by the endless wrangling that they let him have his way. "Corcoran was outnumbered on the Joint Commission, for the rest of the commissioners — including President Rutherford Hayes — were pragmatists who just wanted to finish the monument as soon as possible. [...] After more than a year of this confusion, Corcoran noted disgustedly, the members of Congress became so "wearied with the numerous plans and suggestions of interested parties here" that they finally passed an appropriation to build the obelisk." (Savage, 2009, 126).

Casey's plan was adopted and today's Washington Monument is the result. As of 2015, the marble, granite, and bluestone gneiss structure remains the tallest all-stone structure in the world. Still, the savage bickering over its form and details, and whether it should be built at all, presaged a similarly troubled process when the time arrived for the planning and construction of the Jefferson Memorial. To a degree, this was inevitable, because the site where the Jefferson Memorial now stands had been earmarked at various times for other projects as well, though none of these ever survived beyond the planning stage. It represented one of the prime locations near the White House where an edifice could be placed and still maintain a sense of symmetry and an uncluttered feeling. One of the remaining prime building sites was chosen for the Lincoln Memorial, which was dedicated in 1922.

In 1914, as work on the Lincoln Memorial was being planned and carried out, the idea of a monument to Thomas Jefferson somewhere in the core district of Washington D.C., adjacent in some fashion to the Mall, was first proposed by the Commission of Fine Arts (CFA). This tiny government office, which passes unnoticed by people in the city most of the time, is a fairly influential body in matters related to the aesthetics of government structures in Washington D.C. It was established in 1910 and given further powers by the Shipstead-Luce Act of 1930. Just 4 years after its inception, the CFA was only able to make suggestions, so its members suggested that the Jefferson monument be erected in one of two locations: near the Department of State Building or close to Union Station. Neither location was adopted, and there was no Congressional or Presidential response to the idea at that time, but the idea had at least been floated.

20 years later, during the first presidential term of Franklin Delano Roosevelt, the Jefferson Memorial was revived as a likely and fitting project. The building had been part of the Washington establishment's "to do" list for at least two decades, and it had likely existed before the formal proposal for its creation was made during the first year of World War I. Roosevelt no doubt wished to complete the project as part of his sweeping vision for America, but he also had immediate political reasons for his choice. "By the mid-1930s, when the campaign for the national monument got underway, Franklin Roosevelt and the Democrats saw it as a way to put their imprint on the capital's monumental core, which, until then, had been dominated by Republican plans and Republican heroes. Jefferson was to the Democrats, in effect, what Lincoln was to the Republicans, a patron saint." (Savage, 2009, 244).

As a Democrat taking office at a difficult point in the nation's history, with the Great Depression unfolding thanks to the limitations and problems of the gold standard and an insufficiently bold monetary policy to counteract the collapse, Roosevelt probably wanted a symbol to legitimize his presidency. At least one prominent Republican remembered this fact nine years later when the Memorial was complete and made melodramatic claims that the building represented Roosevelt's intention to establish a Hitler-like dictatorship in America. Regardless, Roosevelt initiated the new project with a letter to Charles Moore, a noted city planner who had joined the CFA in 1915 and subsequently became its Chairman, a position he kept until his retirement in 1937. This letter, which Roosevelt sent in January 1934, brought up the idea of a Jefferson Memorial and asked if a site near the National Archives, which was then undeveloped, was open. Moore replied that the building site the President mentioned was already claimed for the "Apex Building," now dubbed the Federal Trade Commission Building. In suitably courteous terms, he suggested that Roosevelt should address Congress about his project.

Roosevelt took Moore's advice and abandoned his idea of placing the Jefferson Memorial near the National Archives. In fact, he even appeared to play a leading role in beginning construction of the Federal Trade Commission Building. Designed in the Classical Revival style and bearing 10 splendid Art Deco sculptural groups collectively entitled "Man Controlling Trade," the building's creation began in 1938. President Roosevelt came to the site to lay the cornerstone, using the same ceremonial silver trowel George Washington had used to lay the cornerstone of the United States Capitol Building in 1793. Roosevelt also gave a dedication speech, part of which said, "May this permanent home of the Federal Trade Commission stand for all time as a symbol of the purpose of the government to insist on a greater application of the golden rule to the conduct of corporation and business and enterprises in their relationship to the body politic."

Construction of the Apex Building

Modern photo of the building

Though the President abandoned the initial site he had chosen for the Jefferson Memorial, he did not give up his determination to have the monument constructed. As Charles Moore suggested, he put the matter to Congress, and on June 26th, 1934, Congress and the Senate passed a Joint Resolution "authorizing the creation of a Federal Memorial Commission to consider and formulate plans for the construction [...] in the city of Washington, District of Columbia, of a permanent memorial to the memory of Thomas Jefferson, third President of the United States and author of the Declaration of Independence." (73rd Congress, 1934, Chapter 763). This Federal Memorial Commission was to consist of a dozen members, three of whom were to be chosen by President Roosevelt, three picked by the President of the Senate from among serving U.S. Senators, three selected from Congress by the Speaker of the House, and three chosen by the Thomas Jefferson Memorial Foundation, Inc. from among its own members.

The Joint Resolution described the reasons for the Memorial's construction: "[W]hereas there exists no adequate permanent national memorial to Thomas Jefferson in the Nation's Capital; and Whereas the American people feel a deep debt of gratitude to Thomas Jefferson and in honor of the services rendered by him." (73rd Congress, 1934, Chapter 763).

As it turned out, 11 of the Commission's members became a virtual rubber stamp for the decisions of the 12th, a dominating personality with a deep knowledge of the enterprise in which they were engaged. This man was Fiske Kimball, a wide-faced man with penetrating eyes behind wire-rimmed glasses, thick eyebrows, and a heavy mustache. Kimball, always dressed impeccably in three-piece silk suits and neckties, resembled nothing so much as a clever mafia don from a gangster movie, but he was actually one of America's most remarkable architects during the first half of the 20th century, no mean feat when matched against such individuals as Frank Lloyd Wright. His stern mouth and sharp eyes did not conceal a heart of gold and unexpected warmth; those who knew him described him as "brusque, bullish, and profane."

Kimball

Standing over 6 feet tall, Kimball was also described by an acquaintance as a "titan of directed energy," but his architectural knowledge was formidable. Constantly researching and reading at a frantic pace, an effort said to be supported by the excellent and nutritious cooking of his wife Marie, Kimball was a practical architect who worked on many notable projects across the United States. On top of all that, he had been studying about Thomas Jefferson for much of his life, making him ideally suited to the task he was now handed.

As if all that wasn't enough, Jefferson had also been an architect, though in his case the interest was largely amateur (if nevertheless guided by a keen intelligence), and Kimball recognized something of a kindred spirit in Jefferson, at least in the field of building. "In classicism, America was thus not merely a follower; rather a leader in pressing it to its extreme consequences. […] The prophet of the new gospel was Jefferson, its earliest apostles were other distinguished laymen and amateurs. They not only established the ideals, but gave the first object lessons." (Kimball, 1922, 146). Kimball knew Jefferson's architectural theories, concepts, and practices inside out, and he had even written books on the subject, as well as on other architectural topics. As a result, Kimball was intimately familiar with Monticello's architecture, and it would inspire him as he chose the type of building constructed to honor the author of the Declaration of Independence.

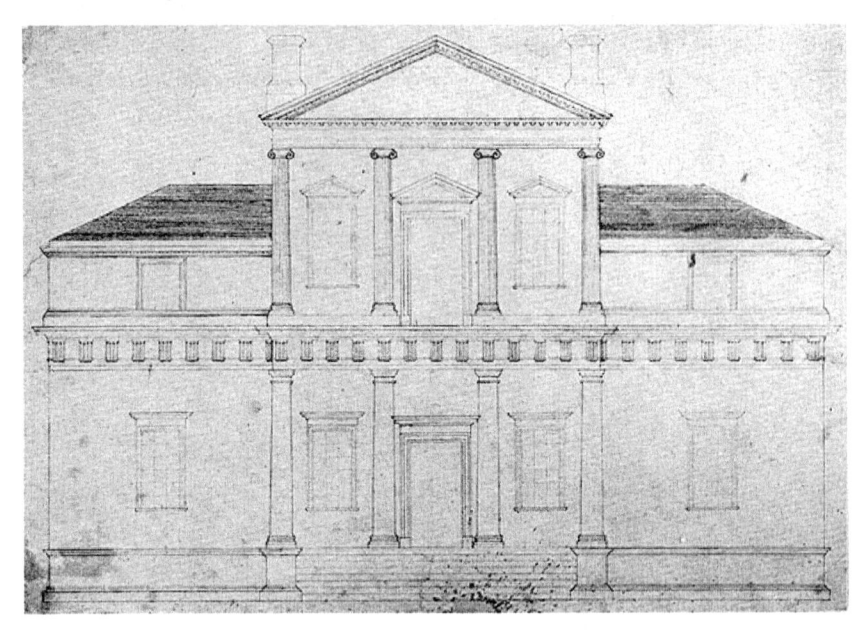

Jefferson's sketch of the design for Monticello appeared in Kimball's *Domestic Architecture of the American Colonies and of the Early Republic* (1922).

Given all of this, Kimball was simply the right man in the right place at the right time, and though he was not the actual designer of the Jefferson Memorial, he was the decisive factor in determining what it would look like and who would carry out the task.

Chapter 3: Starts and Fits

Perhaps not surprisingly, Kimball did not take a modest approach to his assigned work and quickly came up with a bold scheme, in which he "showed himself to be willing to push for an extremely large memorial in a location of great prominence, and suggested the Tidal Basin at the southern end of the White House cross-axis of the Mall, which was the last important site left. He further strongly recommended that the building be a domed Roman hall in deference to

Jefferson's admiration of the Pantheon." (Bedford, 1998, 216).

While Kimball's vision was clear, the plans for the Jefferson Monument were contentious from the start. The CFA, President Roosevelt, and the National Capital Park and Planning Commission all put their seal of approval on the Tidal Basin site, so the location of the Monument was fixed almost from the moment when Kimball chose it. This site, with its flowering cherry trees, would cause a brief but notable incident later when the time came to clear it for construction to begin, but from an early stage, the location appeared to be settled.

An architect named John Russell Pope was subsequently brought in to speak with the Thomas Jefferson Monument Commission. Pope was a highly experienced architect whose excellently planned and executed monuments and public buildings already dotted American cities and the capital itself. His clear grasp of the topic, the breadth of his knowledge, and his authoritative professionalism all compelled the Commission to choose him as the man to actually plan and build the Memorial. Kimball was likely brought on board by Pope's love of the Neoclassical style and deep appreciation of Thomas Jefferson himself, eccentricities which both men shared.

Pope

The National Archives building, one of the buildings designed by Pope

When Pope produced his plans, however, several problems emerged. The first was that the building he planned was immense, meaning it was possibly more than the wet soil at the edge of the Tidal Basin could support. This was an issue similar to that faced by the architects who designed and built the Washington Monument across the Potomac. Even more important, the fact that the projected costs ran over $9 million (approximately $150 million in 2015 dollars) made Congress and Roosevelt skittish, and it led to a demand that the memorial cost no more than $3 million. Pope was somewhat inclined to resist, but Kimball supported the cut and Pope was able to push costs just under $3 million by reducing the dimensions of the building by 20 percent. As it happened, total costs amounted to almost exactly $3 million, indicating the accuracy with which Pope could estimate the price of an architectural project.

The final step taken seemed harmless enough, but it had far-reaching consequences and would cause delays in the beginning of construction. "The National Park Service was then designated as the agency that would oversee the contract. With this last motion, the Thomas Jefferson Memorial Commission concluded its business. By the following day, the design was published in the newspaper, and it was then that the furor began (Bedford, 1998, 220).

Everything had appeared to be quite neatly settled before the public got involved. While laymen may not have been too invested in the details, a small segment of the public, including prominent architects and art critics, believed they were exceptionally qualified to critique and condemn the works of other architects. The Washington newspapers began a chorus of complaints almost immediately, most of which appear rather trivial in retrospect from the perspective of several generations later, but Roosevelt himself was accosted and berated by representatives of the League for Progress in Architecture. One of their complaints was that John Russell Pope had been picked arbitrarily and with no public competition or dialogue, which was to some degree a fair charge.

Some critics also decried the waste of money on the monument at the height of the Great Depression, which was well-meaning but rather misplaced; construction of the Jefferson Monument was the very definition of a "make-work project" that would distribute funds into the economy and stimulate supporting businesses. Furthermore, $3 million, while individually a large sum, was woefully inadequate to even slightly dent the problem of restoring the American economy. What was needed was a strong expansion in the overall money supply, so an expenditure of $3 million on the Jefferson Memorial was meaningless in a macroeconomic sense. It was simply too trivial to make a difference.

Regardless, taking potshots at the proposed Jefferson Memorial became something of a national pastime, perhaps as a way to alleviate general stress over the economic situation in the country. Strident criticism piled up as ever more prominent people and institutions took jabs at the design of the Memorial and the entire overall project. "The faculty of the School of Architecture at Columbia, Pope's alma mater, condemned his design to a Star reporter on 31 March 1937 as a 'lamentable misfit in time and place.' Frank Lloyd Wright, on 30 March 1937, in a letter to President Roosevelt, described the work as an 'arrogant insult to the memory of Thomas Jefferson.'" (Bedford, 1998, 222).

Wright

Pope offered only feeble resistance to these attacks on his ideas; he had been diagnosed with terminal abdominal cancer shortly after he was chosen to head the project and the painful business of dying sapped his ability to handle other matters. Unfortunately, his lack of response was misinterpreted as arrogant disregard for the opinions of the people rather than a byproduct of the fact that he was too ill and exhausted to appear in debate or even muster a letter-writing campaign. As a result, he was castigated even more fervently in the press.

As more and more complaints, each one more frantic than the last, poured into the White House, the House Appropriations Committee decided to suspend the $3 million earmarked for the project. At this juncture, the CFA leveled a final and telling blow by asserting the project was undemocratic and expressed a hidden imperial agenda on Pope's part. Pope was utterly baffled over how to respond to this charge, so he made no statement at all. Congress eliminated the planned funding, effectively suspending the project indefinitely on August 23rd, 1937. Pope died on August 27th, no doubt assuming that his final project would never be completed and instead be relegated to the dustbin of history, where it would soon be forgotten.

Chapter 4: Another Rebellion

Pope may have been too weak to counter his critics, but his widow, Sadie Pope, certainly was not. She began to write numerous letters to President Roosevelt, urging him to use his influence to have the plan carried on, and while she was likely more interested in the project as a memorial to her husband than to Thomas Jefferson, her letters managed to strike a chord. Due in part to her campaign, the project was not completely abandoned but suspended while Roosevelt and his supporters maneuvered to make it workable again.

This proved to be an uphill battle, because the suspension of the original plan allowed for others to fill the void with their own ideas. There was a call from many quarters to make the Thomas Jefferson Memorial a "living memorial," such as a university, hospital, or other building that happened to be named after him. When one Congressman suggested that a planetarium might be a good choice, it triggered a sarcastic response from one of his fellow legislators, who asked, "Why not just adopt the stars as a memorial to Thomas Jefferson?" (Peterson, 1962, 427.).

Even partisan politics offered a few choice quips on the subject. The Republicans, who loathed Roosevelt and New Deal politics, observed at one point that "a New Deal memorial to Jefferson was blasphemous [...] unless he was imaged within 'with tears streaming down his cheeks.'" (Peterson, 1962, 428). Eventually, the CFA was persuaded to call a truce when it was announced that a new open plan would be promised, but to the organization's horror, the plan turned out to be a very slightly modified version of John Russell Pope's much-loathed design. By this point, however, Congress had lost track completely of the complex and esoteric argument, so it voted the $3 million funding back in simply to clear the matter of the Jefferson Memorial off its docket.

Thus, in early 1938, the project had again been given the green light, but after Pope's death, a new architect needed to oversee it. Kimball was part of the Commission itself and therefore could not act as architect as well, so eventually the firm Eggers & Higgins was hired. The company was headed by Otto R. Eggers and Daniel P. Higgins, who were both skilled architects, and the plan was heavily modified by these two men. After surviving more than a year of hostility and argument, including powerful resistance from the CFA, the blueprint was quietly changed by the men hired to carry out the wishes of Pope and his wife Sadie. The results, however, proved both symbolic and attractive, all while retaining several of the features Pope had insisted on most strenuously, such as the low domed roof.

Eggers and Higgins in 1941

With the new plans in hand, the ground was to be prepared in mid-November 1938, readying the building site for the next year. The cornerstone was to be laid in December 1938, after which actual construction was slated to commence in November 1939 and would need to be completed in time for Thomas Jefferson's 200th birthday in April 1943.

A fresh obstacle was waiting in the wings, however, this time from a thoroughly unexpected quarter. The Jefferson Memorial had withstood opposition from the esoteric concerns of the Committee of Fine Arts (CFA) to the personal dislike for the project of certain pundits, but at this point, a strange event that history has dubbed the Cherry Tree Rebellion interrupted work taking place on the Tidal Basin site.

Washington's Tidal Basin was famed then (as it is now) for its flowering cherry trees, a fragrant and beautifully tinted gift from Japan. This magnificent living treasure of the capital was planted just a few years before in 1910. A female world traveler, Eliza Scidmore, visited Japan in the late 19th century and took up the banner of beautifying America's capital with the trees after seeing them in bloom in the Asian nation, which had only recently been opened to Western visitors after a long totalitarian isolation.

Scidmore

Scidmore experienced decades of frustration and failure in her efforts to have cherry trees planted in Washington's public spaces, but she eventually managed to engage Helen Taft, the wife of President William Taft, in her cause as well. Having gained access to the ear of authority, Scidmore was able to arrange the delivery of over 2,000 trees with the assistance of a friendly Japanese official named Jokichi Takamine. Unfortunately, these trees were infested with harmful Japanese insects and tree blight, so President Taft was compelled to order their destruction after reading the report by the Department of Agriculture.

The President was reluctant to take this step, but the resourceful Eliza Scidmore did not abandon the project. With the assistance of the presidential couple, another group of 3,020 cherry trees of a dozen different types – carefully checked this time to ensure the absence of pests and diseases – were imported from Japan. This took place in 1912, just two years after the first disastrous experiment, when "First Lady Helen Taft and the Viscountess Chinda, wife of the Japanese Ambassador, planted the first two Yoshino cherry trees on the north end of the Tidal

Basin." (Garcia, 2012, 1).

The 1912 planting ceremony

The new cherry trees, planted along the shores of the Tidal Basin and at various other prominent locations in the capital, thrived and soon became a much-loved feature of Washington D.C. They were cherished in equal measure for their beauty, their superb fragrance, and the paying tourists they attracted to the city on the Potomac each spring. This gracious and marvelous gift continues to enrich the scene at the capital today, but in 1938, plans were afoot to prepare the ground at the building site beside the Tidal Basin for the Jefferson Memorial's construction and a number of cherry trees stood on this site. To deal with this issue, a plan was arranged to dig the trees up and transplant them to a new location. According to both the Park Service, which was in charge of the actual transplanting, and President Roosevelt, 88 trees were to be excavated and shifted elsewhere. A few of these trees would inevitably die from transplant shock, but every reasonable effort was planned to ensure their successful transfer.

As November 17-19, the days for the transfer, approached, a new figure burst on the scene. This was the owner of the *Washington Times-Herald*, Eleanor Josephine Medill "Cissy" Patterson, whose family fortune enabled her to purchase two of William Hearst's newspapers outright and conglomerate them into the *Times-Herald*. A noted socialite and reporter, Cissy Patterson's dislike of President Roosevelt and her love of Washington's cherry trees – and perhaps a desire to increase the prominence and circulation of her newspaper – induced her into publishing a story about the Jefferson Memorial's construction which could charitably be called exaggerated. Headlines in the *Washington Times-Herald* howled that either 600 or 700 cherry trees were slated to be cut down in order to make room for the Jefferson Memorial, and the real figure of 88 trees was not mentioned since it would likely not mobilize the people.

Patterson

Along with the paper's headlines, Cissy Patterson called on the women of Washington to protest with her at their head, gaining ample publicity for herself in the process, and what ensued was doubtless annoying at the time but provided a moment of comic relief amid the ponderous wrangling of committees and the original architect's death. "Eleanor Patterson's Washington Times and Herald denounced the planners of this project with the same invective these

Republican newspapers habitually used on the New Deal. The destruction of cherry trees, some predicted, would precipitate a diplomatic crisis with Japan." (Peterson, 1962, 430).

A brief and logical consideration of the situation would have revealed, even without further investigation, that Cissy Patterson's claims were monstrously overblown. Around 3,020 cherry trees were present in the capital at the time, so 700 trees would represent 23 percent of the total number. Since the trees were scattered over a number of locations, a building which required the removal of fully 1/4th of Washington's cherry trees would be a colossal structure stretching for miles, necessitating the razing of many buildings as well, perhaps including the White House. The claim was patently absurd on its face, but because the fate of the capital's beloved cherry trees was a deeply emotional issue, logic was swept aside.

The first inkling Roosevelt and the Thomas Jefferson Memorial Commission had that something was amiss came on November 17, 1938, when a band of 50 women appeared at the White House protesting loudly and presenting a petition demanding that the Jefferson Memorial be permanently canceled in order to save the trees. They naturally came away empty-handed, which prompted Patterson to launch the next phase of her campaign. Cissy, "who took daily walks with her poodles under the canopy of the cherry trees" (Klein, 2012, 1), organized a platoon of 150 society ladies on the following day, November 18th, and surviving photographs of the actual Cherry Tree Rebellion protest (some of which appeared in the pages of the *New York Times*) show that these affluent women wore their full-length fur coats, stylish hats, shoes, and dresses, making the procession even more surreal.

Protesters at the Cherry Tree Rebellion

 The engineers and workmen of the Civilian Conservation Corps at the work site were dumfounded and unsure how to respond when 150 angry women in fur coats suddenly swarmed in amongst them. Snatching shovels from the workers' hands, some of the Cherry Tree Rebellion members began to shovel dirt frantically back into the holes around the tree roots, which, if they had paused to reflect, constituted objective proof that the trees were being transplanted and not cut down. The workmen protested loudly but did nothing else, figuring it would be best to await President Roosevelt's intervention after sending messages informing him of the unexpected problem.

 A *New York Times* correspondent who witnessed the protest commented dryly on the society ladies' lack of botanical knowledge, noting that "some of them made a frontal attack on the problem by wresting shovels and picks from workmen who were transplanting a tree at the Tidal Basin. The tree in question, however, turned out to be a long-leaf pine, not a Japanese cherry tree." (New York Times Staff, 1938, 1). Regardless, the women had come prepared, and at one point, they chained themselves to the trees in an effort to stop the work. The *New York Times* photographs of the incident reveal that some of the women were wearing metal cuffs on their wrists, and a few on their ankles, while numerous lengths of steel chain connected them together. Some had draped the chains around their necks as well.

In addition to their efforts to fill in the holes around some cherry trees and deny access to others by chaining themselves in place, the women made melodramatic statements to the reporters attracted by the spectacle and sang songs. The Cherry Tree Rebellion's rallying song was Joyce Kilmer's *Trees*:

> "I think that I shall never see
>
> A poem lovely as a tree.
>
> A tree whose hungry mouth is prest
>
> Against the sweet earth's flowing breast;
>
> A tree that looks at God all day,
>
> And lifts her leafy arms to pray;
>
> A tree that may in summer wear
>
> A nest of robins in her hair;
>
> Upon whose bosom snow has lain;
>
> Who intimately lives with rain.
>
> Poems are made by fools like me,
>
> But only God can make a tree."

The women had even prepared songs of their own, including one which began "Who is it wants these grand old trees displaced? Who is it wants our fair DC disgraced?" (Ruane, 2010, 1). They also made hyperbolic declarations to correspondents. "'This is the worst desecration of beauty in the capital since the burning of the White House by the British,' stated one protestor chained to a tree." (Klein, 2012, 1).

President Roosevelt was working nearby at the White House when the Cherry Tree Rebellion broke out and work on the Jefferson Memorial site came to a halt. Before setting out for the work site to attempt to settle matters, he held a brief press conference with reporters clamoring to know his opinion of this latest development. "The President, who had so far avoided public involvement in the memorial controversy, now made his position absolutely clear. [...] Roosevelt reviewed the stages of the controversy down to the current comic opera finale. 'Well,' he said, 'I don't suppose there is anybody in the world who loves trees quite as much as I do but I recognize that a cherry tree does not live forever.'" (Peterson, 1962, 430).

After making his remarks, Roosevelt set out for the Tidal Basin, and when he arrived, the President surveyed the society ladies in their chains and furs, no doubt glaring haughty defiance at him. He then made a statement to the women, the workmen, and the reporters that mixed matter-of-fact determination with a touch of tongue-in-cheek humor intended to defuse the situation. "The president declared that the trees were going be transplanted, not cut down, and that reports of proposed tree destructions were 'one of the most interesting cases of newspaper flimflam' he had ever encountered. Roosevelt joked that if the protestors didn't leave, 'the cherry trees, the women and their chains would be gently but firmly transplanted in some other part of Potomac Park.'" (Klein, 2012, 1).

Roosevelt then left the scene with the ladies still chained to the trees, but he still had one more arrow in his quiver. Some accounts say that the women unchained themselves shortly thereafter and left of their own accord, deflated by Roosevelt's reasonable stance. The National Park Service, however, preserves a different story, which is perhaps more accurate in light of the fact that the women were likely relishing their sudden fame and thus would've been unwilling to move on account of a few rational and humorous remarks by Roosevelt. According to this tale, Michael Straus, Assistant Secretary of the Interior, was sent to deal with the situation. Combining bluff, everyman good looks with impeccable grooming and authoritative salt-and-pepper hair, Straus was accompanied by servers bearing an ample lunch and a huge quantity of coffee. Straus chatted in personable fashion with the ladies, served them food, and then turned to the refreshing beverages, which soon caused the desired effect. "[A]fter neverending cups of coffee, the ladies' need for restrooms hastened their decision to remove the chains." (Garcia, 2012, 1).

Ultimately, the protesters were removed deftly without the need for threats, arrests, or unpleasantness, and President Roosevelt ordered the rest of the trees to be transplanted in the early morning hours while Cissy Patterson and her platoons of fur-coated advocates were sound asleep in their beds. This proved effective at preventing further interference with the excavation and relocation of the trees, and with that, the Cherry Tree Rebellion was at an end, though it did prompt one more humorous sally by some residents of the capital: "[A] few old Washingtonians started a counter-movement by organizing the 'Chop Down a Cherry Tree Club, Inc.,' which they said was planned primarily to make Washington safe for Washingtonians. George Washington was announced as honorary president, and a hatchet was adopted as the club's emblem." (New York Times Staff, 1938, 1).

Ironically, while Cissy Patterson and her activists were busy protesting the moving of 88 cherry trees from one location to another, the very same Park Service that drew part of their wrath was preparing plans to plant an additional 1,000 Japanese cherry trees in the capital to increase its beauty and ensure that a robust, healthy population of the popular living landmarks would continue into the future.

Chapter 5: Construction of the Jefferson Memorial

Pictures of the Jefferson Memorial under construction

After all the hassles and the bizarre protests were in the past, the construction of the Jefferson Memorial officially began in December 1938 with the ceremonial laying of the cornerstone by President Roosevelt. In a strange (and ultimately futile) gesture, the CFA actually paid to have a pamphlet published and distributed repeating all the earlier attacks on the Memorial, adding an extra declaration that the Tidal Basin site was unsuitable due to the fact that it contradicted a 1792 plan for keeping that particular stretch of waterside open and undeveloped. By this time, however, the pamphlet had no practical effect whatsoever. It is difficult to guess whether the CFA members hoped the partially constructed building would be disassembled as the President and Congress suddenly caved in to their complaints or if they merely wanted the satisfaction of being able to say they had warned everyone when the Jefferson Memorial collapsed, proved to be the center of a Roosevelt dictatorship, or blighted the Washington cherry trees forever.

Whatever the case, when the ceremonial laying of the cornerstone took place on December 15th, 1938, about 300 people gathered to witness the event, including both government officials and curious members of the public, not to mention the inevitable squadron of reporters.

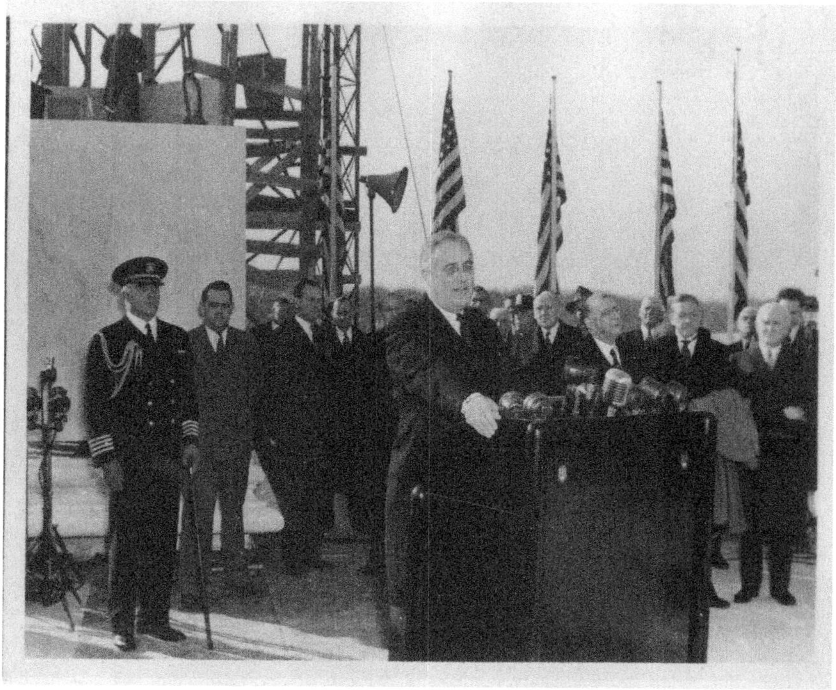

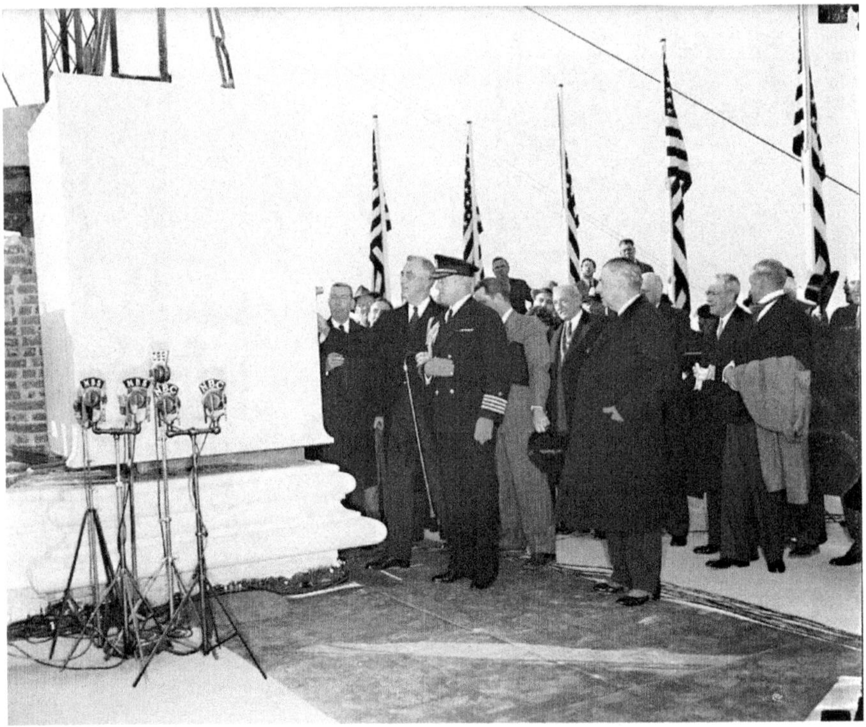

Pictures of Roosevelt at the ceremony laying the cornerstone of the Jefferson Memorial

By this time, Fiske Kimball, his work completed, had stepped down as the head of the Thomas Jefferson Memorial Commission and was replaced by Stuart G. Gibboney. Gibboney, founder of the Thomas Jefferson Foundation, was a tireless enthusiast for all things Jefferson and had managed at one point to collect $1 million in private donation for the restoration and preservation of Monticello.

As the newly appointed Chairman of the Thomas Jefferson Memorial Commission, Gibboney was present when Roosevelt prepared to lay the cornerstone, but rather than lay the cornerstone personally, the president handed the shovel to Gibboney and requested that he move the first shovelfuls of earth in Roosevelt's name, a gesture which was undoubtedly much appreciated by the zealous Jeffersonian. After Gibboney had carried out the ritual commencement of the construction work, Roosevelt made a short address to the gathered spectators in which he described how the Jefferson Memorial would complete the central monumental core of Washington D.C., which was based around two axes forming a large cross. The long axis ran from the Capitol Building through the Washington Monument and ended at the Lincoln

Memorial on the banks of the Potomac River. The short axis ran from the White House through the Washington Monument (the center of the cruciform plan) and ended at the Tidal Basin. The point where the cornerstone of the Jefferson Memorial had just been laid was at this end of the short axis, so the construction of the Memorial would complete the symmetrical arrangement of Washington landmarks neatly.

The Washington Monument from the Jefferson Memorial

Picture of the Lincoln Memorial, Washington Monument, and Capitol

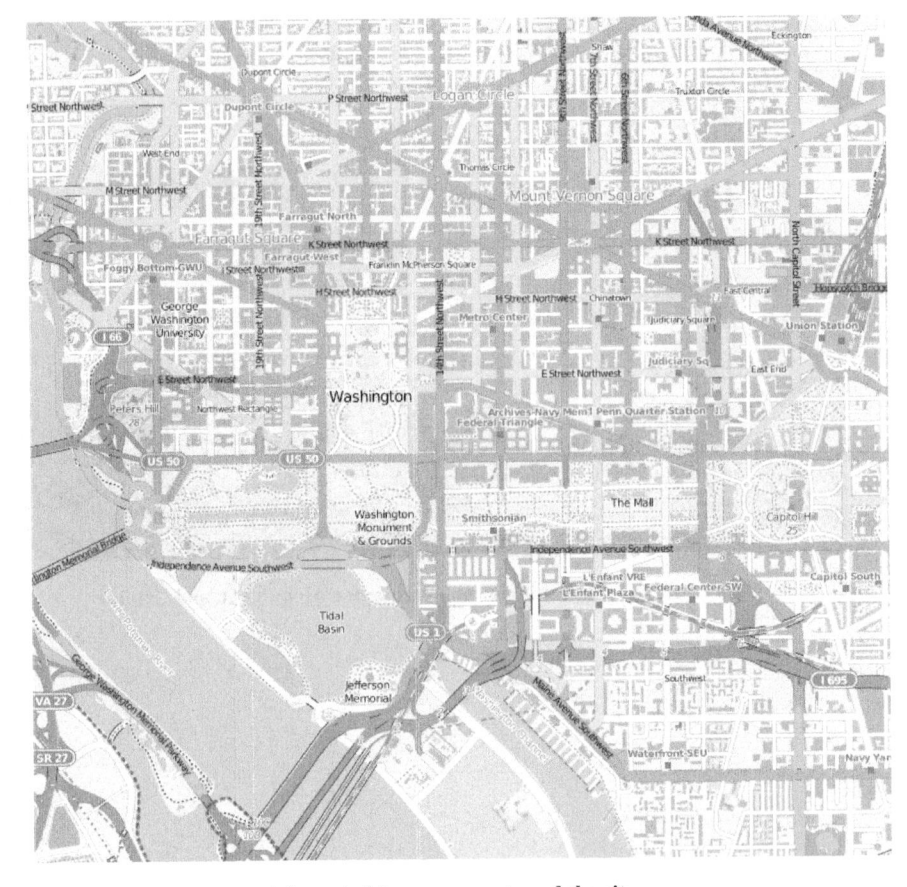

A layout of the monuments and the city

Roosevelt then went on to praise the accomplishments of Thomas Jefferson and laud his 50 years of service to the United States of America. Applause greeted the end of the president's speech, and the construction of the Jefferson Memorial had, at long last, been launched.

Originally conceived in 1914, the monument was finally starting to take material shape a generation later. The completed building stands on a pair of circular concentric terraces, with the outer measuring a full 422 feet in diameter. It is marked by a 3 foot high granite retaining wall. The second, inner terrace is likewise circular and features a 10 foot marble retaining wall. The diameter of this section is 294 feet, and overall, the two terraces lift the base of the Jefferson Memorial 25 feet above the surrounding ground. Overall, the edifice is approximately 120 feet tall.

This picture from inside shows the structure's two-terraced format.

The main entrance was built on the north side of the structure and features a portico decorated with sculptured pediment. 40 foot high columns surround both the inner and outer walls, and the thick walls support the dome, which is double shelled. The outer shell is reinforced by a massive structural steel skeleton, but the inner shell supports itself, with the tension of stone against stone sufficient to keep it in place.

Christopher Hollis' picture of the columns

Jamie Adams' picture of the steps and portico

Jamie Adams' picture of the dome

Many different types of stone were used in the construction, which was conducted under the direction of Eggers and Higgins. These include Missouri gray marble for the pedestal, Georgian white marble for the interior walls, exterior columns and walls cut from Vermont-quarried Danby Imperial marble (which is also used for the dome), a pink Tennessee marble floor, and an Indiana limestone portico vault. The stone was chosen for its appearance and construction qualities but also to represent various symbolic portions of American history. The use of Vermont and Georgia marble, for example, were picked to represent the two major regional divisions of the original 13 colonies: the North and the South. Indiana and Tennessee were among the first states to be added to the United States, and thus stones from there were selected as emblematic of westward expansion. Finally, the Minnesota granite and Missouri marble come from states created out of the Louisiana Purchase, a territorial expansion of 828,000 square miles in the nation's heartland which was carried out by Jefferson as president.

Though the building itself was made with the utmost skill and precision and has needed little work in the years since it was erected, a testament to the skills of Pope, Eggers, and Higgins as architects, the ground it stands on has required stabilization once in the days since then. Standing on the slightly marshy ground near the verge of the Tidal Basin, the Jefferson Monument represents a weight of many tens of thousands of tons, even though this mass is well-distributed thanks to its double terraced design. In 1968, the director of the National Park Service, George B. Hartzog Jr., testified before a House Appropriations subcommittee on the risk that the Jefferson Memorial might eventually slide off its base and collapse into the Tidal Basin if the foundation was not stabilized with additional subterranean buttresses and rafts. Though many years would need to pass before such a drastic event became even slightly possible, Hartzog deemed it best to make the necessary reinforcements while the building was still completely sound and the detectable shifting was limited to a few inches. Thus, he asked for $1.2 million to make the necessary stabilizing improvements. This request was granted, and the Jefferson Memorial was closed temporarily to the public in October 1969 to enable workmen and architects to carry out the changes Hartzog had outlined.

Hartzog

The process required a full 11 months to complete, but it represented a major, permanent improvement to the Memorial's overall stability. The Memorial was reopened to the public on September 5, 1970, and as of 2015, this remains the longest period during which the Jefferson Memorial was closed to public access. It was also the most expensive repair conducted on the structure to date.

Hartzog became Director of the National Park Service in 1964 and was initially hailed for his energy and vision. He contributed to America's national park and monument riches by opening some 62 new parks and carrying out a vigorous program of historical restoration. Eventually, he sacrificed his job in order to provide the park system with the funding he believed it merited in order to supply quality public parks and monuments to the American people. This all occurred simultaneously with the repairs to the Jefferson Memorial's foundations, and in 1969, when the Park Service's funding was cut, Hartzog responded by informing the Nixon administration and Stewart Udall, Secretary of the Interior that it would be impossible to keep all public parks open on the reduced budget. To pressure the administration into raising the budget again, he earmarked two of the nation's most popular locales, the Grand Canyon and the Washington Monument, for twice a week closures into the indefinite future. The administration responded by providing the full funding necessary to keep the public park and monument system operational at a high level of quality and service. Hartzog's actions entered the lexicon as the "Washington Monument Syndrome," a tactic that relies on closing popular public facilities to pressure the federal government and effectively obtain monetary concessions from Congress.

Hartzog was relieved of his post in 1972, as he had anticipated prior to beginning his maneuver, but by then, he had achieved his goals. America's parks were fully funded, and the Jefferson Memorial now possessed a greatly improved foundation which would sustain it for many decades to come.

Chapter 6: The Statue of Jefferson

Jamie Adams' picture of the Jefferson statue

Standing 19 feet high and weighing 5 tons, the statue of Thomas Jefferson in the Jefferson

Memorial is a looming presence visible from the exterior through the screen of columns. This statue was created by the noted sculptor Rudolph Evans to serve as the site's centerpiece, and the master craftsman used a simple but effective formulation of 90% copper and 10% tin to prepare the bronze from which the final statue was cast. Though the Memorial was dedicated and opened to the public in 1943, it was not until 1947 that the actual bronze statue was set up inside; during the intervening four years, a plaster duplicate stood in its place and was colored to resemble bronze.

The statue's design and sculptor were chosen via competitive submissions. The matter of how to design a suitable statue as the finishing touch for the Memorial was first mulled by the Committee on Sculpture, which prepared a report to submit to the Thomas Jefferson Memorial Commission. This report, handed over on April 3, 1939 to the Memorial Commission, suggested that a public call for competitive entries, supported by photographs of the artists' previous work, should be made. The Memorial Commission readily adopted this suggestion, and the group which was to review the applications and pick the best consisted of four men. One of these was Fiske Kimball himself. The second was Henri Gabriel Marceau, an architect and art historian who was later Director of the Philadelphia Museum of Art and a close friend of associate of Kimball. The third member was James Earle Fraser, a sculptor who designed the famous Indian Head Nickel with its reverse image of a buffalo, as well as the world-renowned sculpture "End of the Trail," which depicts a defeated yet noble Native American lancer. The last man on the jury was Heinz Warneke, a sculptor specializing in animal depictions.

In all, 101 entries were received with the correct documentation. Out of these, six finalists were selected, and two men were chosen from among these to carry out two separate tasks. The sculptor Rudulph Evans was picked to make the colossal statue of Jefferson himself, which was to stand at the Memorial's center, and Adolph A. Weiman was chosen to create the pediment sculpture above the entrance portico. "Carved in marble above the entranceway is a massive sculptured group, the work of Adolph A. Weiman, depicting Jefferson and four other members of the committee that drafted the Declaration of Independence: John Adams, Benjamin Franklin, Roger Sherman, and Robert Livingstone. The sculpture is modeled from a painting of the committee presenting the Continental Congress with the Declaration of Independence." (Ferry, 2003, 33).

Once World War II was over, it was possible to use large quantities of metal for peacetime purposes again, and the creation of the massive Jefferson statue began in earnest. The Roman Bronze Company of Corona, New York was tabbed to carry out the actual casting of this titanic piece thanks to its magnificent work in creating the bronze statue "Lincoln the Frontiersman" for the Ewa Plantation School on the island of Oahu in the state of Hawaii. This statue shows the beardless young Lincoln, axe in hand, in a dynamic pose atop cut stumps and logs. The sculptor, Avard T. Fairbanks, had chosen to depict Lincoln as "'powerful, alert, aggressive,' and with eyes through which Lincoln visualized far ahead to the blessings of 'a free and united nation.'"

(Fairbanks, 2005, 49). The Roman Bronze Company had reproduced Fairbanks' statue so faithfully that it was chosen to make the Jefferson statue as well at a total cost of $21,104 (approximately $230,000 in 2015 dollars).

The huge statue was cast in 21 sections and then assembled to produce the final result. It was placed flat on its back in a truck and driven from Corona to the Jefferson Memorial site, arriving at 10:00 in the morning on Tuesday, April 22, 1947. The Memorial was closed and a temporary ramp was built inside to install the statue while the plaster substitute was sectioned and removed. The statue was moved to a vertical position on Thursday, April 24, and was fully installed on its plinth by the late evening of Saturday, April 26. The Memorial was reopened to the public the next day. "Most visitors might not notice the difference. The plaster figure was painted a dull bronze color looking reasonably metallic. But to Gus Panknen, head guard at the Memorial, the difference is between 'a diamond and a piece of glass.'" (NYT Special, 1947, 25).

The installation of the statue in 1947

The giant statue of Thomas Jefferson stands on a polished, hexagonal plinth of dark stone which rises in three tiers from the floor. Like several structures in the capital, this plinth is actually made from stone quarried far away in the Upper Midwest, in this case the "Arrowhead" region of Northern Minnesota. The stone is called "Mesabi Black granite," but it is actually layered gabbro, a kind of volcanic rock that forms in magma chambers deep underground. This gabbro was brought close to the surface along Lake Superior's north shore by the tilting of stone layers during geologic processes, part of the Duluth Complex of volcanic rocks. In other words, the stone that Jefferson's statue now stands on was formed by volcanic activity some 1.1 billion years ago, and the rock formations around Lake Superior have supplied several different kinds of high quality stone for Washington D.C. projects; for example, the Department of the Interior Building includes high quality brownstone quarried in the early 20th century by the Lake Superior Brownstone company of Port Wing, a small town located in the remote northern parts of Wisconsin.

The open views from the Jefferson Memorial, the bold and confident statue of the Founder created by Rudulph Evans, and the selected passages from Jefferson's works inscribed on the walls, glorying in American freedom and casting eternal defiance in the teeth of despots, continued the tradition of celebrating the United States' space and energy through the monuments of the past. "John Russell Pope's temple form [...] was [...] less a hushed space for psychological engagement than a platform to inspire the mind to soar. The statue by Rudulph Evans adhered to the conventional nineteenth-century hero formula: a standing figure in period costume holding an important document in his hand, in this case the Declaration of Independence. On the walls and cornice surrounding the statue appear excerpts from Jefferson's writings, cherry-picked to put his thoughts and achievements in the most favorable light." (Savage, 2009, 244).

Naturally, the quotes contain excerpts from the Declaration of Independence, including the famous phrase "life, liberty, and pursuit of happiness," an appeal for religious freedom, thoughts on the implications of no taxation without representation, a passionate denunciation of the degrading effects of slavery on both master and slave (which was likely not intended to be hypocritical despite Jefferson's own slave-owning because he believed the institution would soon fade), and musings on the necessity of eventually updating laws to changed circumstances (but to do so with care and only when strictly necessary). The quotes are rendered visible by individually cast bronze letters inlaid into the walls.

Billy Hathorn's picture of one of the passages

Most prominent of all is a quote in gigantic letters that runs in a band around the rotunda's dome, though in this case no bronze is used as a highlight. This quotation reads, "I have sworn upon the altar of God eternal hostility against every form of tyranny over the mind of man."

Chapter 7: The Dedication of the Jefferson Memorial

Once the final stones were laid and the tools and paraphernalia of building were cleared away, it was necessary to carry out a suitable dedication ceremony to mark the Jefferson Memorial as a national shrine of the American republic. Fittingly, the date picked for this ritual event was April 13, 1943, the 200th anniversary of Thomas Jefferson's birth. The weather was cold and foul, but President Roosevelt, despite his ailing condition, carried out the dedication nevertheless, abandoning the wheelchair he so often used. For the ceremony, the actual Declaration of Independence was brought to the Memorial and placed at the feet of Jefferson's statue in a specially constructed shatterproof case. The priceless document was protected by a detachment of 18 Marines in dress uniform but armed with Thompson submachine guns with live ammunition supplied on the remote chance that German infiltrators tried to kill Roosevelt or steal or destroy the Declaration of Independence. These "Tommy guns" used box magazines rather than the drum magazines made famous by countless gangster movies, making them more maneuverable.

Meanwhile, the area around the Memorial, as well as the route leading from the White House to the shores of the Tidal Basin, were swarming with police from the Washington D.C. police department, armed Secret Service men, and a number of military police from the U.S. Army equipped with M1 rifles with fixed bayonets. If a dramatic attempt to assassinate the American President had been made, the assassins would not have found the Americans unprepared.

A dense throng of hundreds was gathered at the Jefferson Memorial to witness or participate in the dedication ceremony, and finally, it was time for Franklin D. Roosevelt himself to put in an appearance. "The blossoms of Washington's famous cherry trees were rather the worse for recent high winds and sharp weather as the President's procession drove slowly under the grayish skies to the memorial, which takes its place as one of the capital's leading architectural adornments. […] The Marine Band played "Hail to the Chief" as the President, wearing a black cape over his gray business suit, appeared on the speakers' stand, which was covered by a red, white, and blue canopy." (Shalett, 1943, 16).

Many foreign and domestic dignitaries were present, including Crown Princess Martha, a member of the Norwegian royalty, and United Nations representatives. An ecumenical note was struck by the presence of both an Episcopalian and a Catholic bishop to pronounce the appropriate blessings, and the Star Spangled Banner was performed by Grace Moore, a Metropolitan Opera soprano famed for her role as Louise in the opera of the same name by Gustave Charpentier.

In keeping with the wartime atmosphere, the conclusion of President Roosevelt's speech struck a rather somber and martial note: "He proved that the seeming eclipse of liberty can prove to be the dawn of more liberty. Those who fight the tyranny of our own time will come to learn that lesson. Among all the peoples of the earth, the cruelties and oppressions of its would-be masters have taught this generation what liberties can mean. This lesson, so bitterly learned, will never be forgotten while this generation lives. [...] I have sworn upon the altar of God eternal hostility against every form of tyranny over the mind of man." (Shalett, 1943, 1).

A picture from the dedication event

At the same time that Roosevelt was finishing his speech with the same quote from Jefferson inscribed on the rotunda above him, Justice Felix Frankfurter was giving a speech at the Library of Congress on the subject of the Jefferson bicentennial. Denouncing everything from radios, magazines, and newspapers to movies, the overexcited Justice leveled a final barb at the Jefferson Memorial, the New Deal, and President Roosevelt himself when he declared that the Administration was following a "pattern" that would lead to a dictatorial fascist regime utterly indistinguishable from that of Hitler's in Germany.

As the controversial history of the Memorial and the dedication day's events all suggest, the Jefferson Memorial was a curious phenomenon, and it remained so. It had been desired for many years, but when it began to emerge into reality, it was subjected to an endless torrent of essentially hollow but extremely bombastic and zealous criticism, including the final indirect insult from Justice Frankfurter, who clearly felt it was a monument to Roosevelt's ambitions. However, now that the debates are long past, the debaters are long dead, and the Jefferson Memorial stands complete, it is difficult to argue with Fiske Kimball's statement regarding his preference for the Neoclassical style when building the great monument: "The triumph of literal classicism in 1825, with its ideal formal schemes of temple and rotunda, had been prepared by Jefferson's prophetic insistence on these very types, from the time of the Revolution itself. […] Criticism of such buildings from a functional viewpoint is irrelevant […] there can be no doubt that they endowed America with an architectural tradition unsurpassed in the qualities of monumentality and dignity." (Kimball, 1922, 260).

Subsequent generations of Washington inhabitants have viewed the Memorial in a very different light, and as a symbol of Jefferson watching over the republic he helped found. The Memorial is said to give the spirit of Jefferson a material presence in the capital of the United States, as President Ronald Reagan underlined: "'Presidents know about this, too,' Reagan said. Jefferson was a permanent guardian over his successors, for 'directly down the lawn and across the Ellipse from the White House are those ordered, classic lines of the Jefferson Memorial and the eyes of the 19-foot statue that gaze directly into the White House, a reminder to any of us who might occupy that mansion of the quality of mind and generosity of heart that once abided there and has been so rarely seen there again.'" (Meacham, 2012, 503).

Standing on its two concentric circular terraces, mirrored in the Tidal Basin, and surrounded by the flowering cherry trees Cissy Patterson and her Cherry Tree Rebellion had feared it would eradicate, the Memorial is a remarkable testament to how a beautiful and significant structure can emerge even out of a process rife with petty and irrational human squabbling. The architect who designed this now-classic Washington D.C. building, John Russell Pope, died at the early age of 63 just four days after the project had apparently been scuttled in 1937, never to realize that his creation would become an actual national landmark. The modernist CFA made hysterical claims that the Memorial's style marked the end of democracy and the beginning of a Hitler-like dictatorship in the United States, while President Roosevelt struck the opposite note when he spoke at the building's dedication on April 13, 1943. "Standing bare-headed before the three-million-dollar marble shrine on the shore of the wind-whipped Tidal Basin, Mr. Roosevelt […] vigorously voiced agreement with the third President that 'men are capable of their own government.' 'No king, no tyrant, no dictator can govern for them as wisely as they can govern for themselves,' he proceeded, noting that he echoed a belief of Jefferson." (Shalett, 1943, 1).

The complaints leveled at the Jefferson Memorial during the first half of the 20th century seem strange and remote to modern ears, but controversy still clings to the Memorial. In the 21st century, the political and cultural cognoscenti of the United States decry the monument as the celebration of a hypocrite, a man who spoke thunderous words of freedom while enriching himself through the labor of slaves.

Considering the hatred directed at it both before and after its construction, it is perhaps remarkable that the Jefferson Memorial ever achieved physical reality in the first place. At the same time, it is also somewhat fitting that the elegant neoclassical temple's history is be as complicated and nuanced as that of the man whose memory it recalls: the Enlightenment scholar who was paradoxically both a slave-owner and the writer of the Declaration of Independence, a document destined to found a country that proved for the first time that a vast and diverse nation, and not merely a tiny homogeneous city-state, could house and maintain a successful republic based on liberty.

Robert J. Boser's picture of the Jefferson Memorial from the Washington Monument

Bibliography

73rd Congress, Session II. *Joint Resolution, Chapter 763, June 26th, 1934.* Washington D.C., 1934. Available online at http://legisworks.org/congress/73/pubres-49.pdf .

Bedford, Steven McLeod. *John Russell Pope: Architect of Empire.* New York City, 1998.

Fairbanks, Eugene. "Sculptural Commemorations of Abraham Lincoln by Avard T. Fairbanks." *Journal of the Abraham Lincoln Association.* Volume 26, Issue 2, Summer 2005: 49 – 74. Print.

Ferry, Joseph. *The Jefferson Memorial.* Stockton, 2003.

Garcia, JoAnn. "Cherry Tree Rebellion." *Ranger Journal.* National Park Service, 15 Mar. 2012. Web. 29 Jan. 2015. http://www.nps.gov/nama/blogs/Cherry-Tree-Rebellion.htm

Kimball, Fiske. *Domestic Architecture of the American Colonies and of the Early Republic.* New York City, 1922.

Klein, Christopher. "The Drama Behind 100 Years of Washington's Cherry Blossoms." *History in the Headlines.* History Channel website, 20 Mar. 2012. Web. 29 Jan. 2015.

http://www.history.com/news/the-drama-behind-100-years-of-washingtons-cherry-blossoms

Meacham, John. *Thomas Jefferson: The Art of Power.* New York City, 2012.

Mitchell, Thomas G. *Antislavery Politics in Antebellum and Civil War America.* Westport, 2007.

New York Times staff. "Roosevelt Curbs Tree 'Rebellion.'" *New York Times.* 19 Nov. 1938: 1. Print.

Peterson, Merrill D. *The Jefferson Image in the American Mind.* New York City, 1962.

Ruane, Michael E. "Some cherry trees gave their lives for Jefferson Memorial." *Breaking News Blog.* The Washington Post online, 28 Mar. 2010. Web. 29 Jan. 2015.

http://www.washingtonpost.com/wp-dyn/content/article/2010/03/27/AR2010032701305.html

Savage, Kirk. *Monument Wars: Washington, D.C., the National Mall, and the Transformation of the Memorial Landscape.* Los Angeles, 2009.

Shalett, Sidney. "Roosevelt, Hailing Jefferson, Looks to Gain in Liberty." *New York Times.* 14 Apr. 1943: 1, 16. Print.

Special to the New York Times. "Bronze Jefferson Placed in Capital." *New York Times.* 30 Apr. 1947: 25. Print.

Made in the USA
Middletown, DE
05 September 2021